Breaking

Through

Barriers

A collection of short stories from powerful, courageous, and determined women

Presented by Author:

Tanicia

"Shamay Speaks"

Currie

Published by Shamay Speaks

www.ShamaySpeaks.com

Book cover designed by Shauny B with KnockSmith Productions
www.knocksmithmagazine.com

Printed in the United States of America

ISBN: 978-0-9966729-1-7

Dedication

I dedicate this book to all the women who have stepped out of their comfort zone and took a chance by following their dreams. I also dedicate this book to the single mothers out there who never give up on their goals. I thank all the women who believed in me to lead them during their journey to authorship.

Synopsis:

Breaking Through Barriers is a collection of short stories from powerful, courageous, and determined women who are ready to spread their message. This book features amazing women from different walks of life, who have gained strength and wisdom from their past while learning to move forward. The book's visionary, Tanicia "Shamay Speaks" Currie, believes that God has the power to turn your "mess" into a MESSage and that we all have a story that can provide someone with insight, inspiration, and motivation. Being a three time author herself, Tanicia believes that writing your story can be the first step to healing and overcoming your past experiences as she feels her first published book served as her therapy process.

About the visionary "Shamay Speaks"

Tanicia "Shamay Speaks" Currie is a single mother with a full time job, who does not believe in settling in life. Having faced many life challenges, including having three heart surgeries in just 32 years, Tanicia feels that God definitely gave her a purpose. Growing up in a challenging environment with a drug addiction in her home, she convinced herself that there had to be more to life than those circumstances. Rather than allow her upbringing to dictate her success, she decided to turn her life's hardships into motivation to persevere in life. She became the first in her immediate family to graduate college with a Bachelor's degree. In 2009, she went on to open Cause' N A Stir Entertainment, hosting events from concerts to fashion shows to annual toy drives. Her life changed in 2013 when her daughter Laniyah was born. Laniyah is the best blessing she ever received, but becoming a mother also showed her that it was time to kick life into overdrive. Tanicia is currently the CEO of Branches of Community Services, which helps her give back to those in need. In 2014, she decided to finish the book she started over 8 years prior. She published her first book titled *"Deep Within I Knew He Wasn't for Me* in October 2015. Tanicia is a featured author in two empowerment books *Igniting The Vision* and *Stand Up Be Heard.* Her next book will release early 2017. Being passionate about empowering others to rise above their circumstances and take charge of their destiny, Tanicia's mission in life is to chase all that life has to offer, never give up, and stay humble. Tanicia truly hopes to use her life story, books, videos, events, and speaking to inspire others to follow their dreams despite their circumstances. Tanicia's theme for 2016 is "Speak Upward Shift Upward!" Tanicia looks forward to leaving an empowering legacy for her daughter, as well as, enjoying the extraordinary journey that God has laid out for her!

Tanicia "Shamay Speaks" Currie's vision:

Assisting others in truly understanding they deserve the absolute BEST in life, business, and relationships.

Table of Contents

Introduction
by Shamay Speaks:

I want to start by saying when you become sure and serious about what you desire in your life and you put God first, the blessings will start to line up right before your eyes. In my first 33 years of life I have struggled to understand my purpose. After graduating college and working in my major field for a year, I knew I wanted to be my own boss but living my "purpose" was something totally different. I have done many things in life and have overcome so much. I could sit here and talk about all the things I have been through and overcame but my favorite quote my uncle Walter says is, "I've had it better than some and worse than others." One thing I do know, and what it took some time to discover is, I have a purpose in this world, as each of us does. My whole life I have been a person that people would always call for advice and resources, etc. Within the last two years I have gone from being a single mother working two part-time jobs making less than $1000.00 monthly, to becoming a three-time author, opening a non-profit, being featured on TV shows, and so much more. I say that to say, I firmly believe you can shift your mindset to change your life. My mindset has shifted so much. I believe my mess was designed to be turned into a message, to show other women that you can overcome hardship and even help others. Even though the things I went through didn't feel like a MESSage at the time, I trust that God had a purpose in it all.

During the last two years, especially after I released my first book, many women asked me how I did it. I was already wondering how I could help other women go to the next level in life. I met with my life/business coach Sheya Chisenga and made many plans for 2016. Shortly after I met with her, I thought about joining another book compilation. I had already been a co-author in two other amazing book compilations at that point. I started thinking about and remembering that my purpose was, and is, still being defined. I gave myself one weekend to think about everything and I truly feel God placed this project on my heart. It was like some powerful thoughts came to me all at once, and I said to myself, "that's it, I am going to create a book compilation to help other women spread their message and accomplish their goals." Within two days I had a complete plan for this project and I added workshops to help assist these amazing women on their own self-publishing journey. Being that I was already a self-published author and had done much of the research on my own; I thought it would be so awesome to be the support the ladies needed to accomplish their goal of becoming a published author. I also thought about how awesome it would be to assist women with sharing their story because we all have a story inside of us that can help another person. However, no one will know our stories and their power if we don't share them. With that being said, I am truly excited! Let me tell you, you will know when you are walking in your purpose because you will get these surges of positive energy when you are on the right path. I believe those are part of the signs that God gives you when your purpose is being fulfilled. I truly know that from my life, the good and the bad, that God has a true purpose for me. Keep in mind, when you become committed to controlling your destiny and you shift your mindset upward, you can break through any of life's barriers. My mission is to inspire and empower women by the masses to understand that they deserve the absolute BEST in life, business, and relationships! I truly thank every amazing woman who believed in me enough to allow me to assist them in accomplishing their goal of becoming an author. You ladies can break through any barriers and lives will be changed from your stories and your courage. God bless you all on this success journey and everything you decided to do in life. May you continue to walk by faith, not by sight.

To start the book, I decided to list some of the life and success tips I have truly learned within the last two years that have led me here. God has transformed my life and my mind. In two years, I have been an author three times, opened a non-profit, have been featured in newspapers, magazines, and local TV shows. Trust that you can change your mindset and change your life, and that we all have a message another can learn from.

12 Life and Success Tips: (Some of what I have learned thus far):

1) Know your worth and understand that you deserve the BEST in life, business, and relationships. Worth translates into your confidence.

2) No matter what you have been through, no matter your upbringing, it does not define you.

3) Set a goal to be better than you were yesterday. Change doesn't happen overnight and neither does healing past hurts. So be very careful to not let your past outshine your future.

4) Being broke is a mindset. Also remember some people have broken mindsets so they will not understand your vision and that's okay!

5) Be unapologetic about your success and accomplishments; don't dim your light for anyone.

6) Baby steps are fine. Remember a step not taken is an opportunity missed.

7) As Caterina Rando says, "DONE is better than perfect." So be willing to just go for it and learn as you go. Life is trial and error.

8) To be successful, you must be willing to sacrifice and step out your of comfort zone. There's rarely success with staying in your comfort zone.

9) Seek a mentor or life/business coach. Yes, getting help and support is okay because if you could have done it alone, you would have done it by now.

10) Actions speak louder than words; don't be a talker, be a doer!

11) The only failures are quitters so you will never know your potential if you quit before you begin.

12) As my Pastors Shantell and Damon Owens said, "be a frog not a grasshopper." Grasshoppers stay in the grass, frogs leap; so are you going to stay stuck in the grass like a grasshopper or leap into your destiny?

Healing
And
Forgiveness

"Breaking through Barriers" Book Visionary:

Tanicia "Shamay Speaks" Currie

Age 33

East Bay Area, Ca

Mother-Author-Empowerment Coach-Speaker-Event Planner-Entrepreneur

www.ShamaySpeaks.com

"Accountability then Forgiveness then Healing is Where True Growth Occurs"

Have you ever felt those feelings of "why me?" Have you harbored anger and disappointment within you? Have you had a situation happen to you and you felt like you didn't deserve it? Well that's how I felt when I found out I was pregnant. It wasn't that I was disappointed with having a child but rather disappointed with myself for not following my heart and with the outcome of this relationship situation. I found out I was pregnant within seven days of finding out my daughter's father was not who he portrayed himself to be, which was one month after I decided to stop dating him due to my women's intuition. There were so many feelings that I was dealing with and having pregnancy hormones didn't help. A child is a blessing and pregnancy is supposed to be a happy time; however, I felt angry, disappointed, sad, heartbroken, betrayed, confused, and stuck. After I saw my little baby's two hands and two feet, I felt happy, but it seemed I found out new surprises about her father monthly.

In my first book *Deep Within I Knew He Wasn't For Me*, I discuss my relationship experiences, including my pregnancy; however, I want to focus more on how I was able to get to the happy point that I am at in life now. When you're faced with everything that I was dealing with sometimes you don't know how to feel, especially when things appear as if you will be a single parent and be alone forever. Being a single parent was always a fear of mine because I wanted marriage before children. I also didn't want to repeat my upbringing, but that's another story. Everything that happened during the first five months of my pregnancy was enough to make me not trust anyone for a whole lifetime. I am thankful that I am the kind of woman who will make things happen. I knew my baby would be provided for no matter what I needed to do. I was also fortunate to have been able to acquire resources to help me with my baby, as well as, have the support of family and friends.

During my pregnancy my feelings were up and down and my baby's father was not my favorite person either. The way things were going with my daughter's father, all the drama, finding out more crazy information about him, and the fact that I was going to have to deal with him forever were not the most fun things to deal with. I was very stressed and I couldn't stand him. It didn't make it any better that I have had 3 heart surgeries; therefore, stress is not good for my health at all. I spent a lot of time crying and being angry during the early months of my pregnancy.

The realization:

One day, after coming from my finding out the sex of my baby, which I was excited about, I discovered some news that further broke my heart and angered me. I learned my daughter's father had another child on the way. This was on top of all of the madness that I was dealing with, such as hearing lies from a grown woman he was dealing with (not the other one who was pregnant either). What grown woman lies about a man who's dogging her? I didn't know what about the situation was true; the only thing I knew that was truth was that I was having a baby in less than four months.

I remember being at work and having to leave work because I was in tears. I thought, "What else could happen?" I came home, sat on my porch, and cried. Now I had increased feelings of anger, sadness, distrust, and more disappointment within myself. Abortion even crossed my mind, but I was almost five months. Plus I told myself I would never have an abortion. Again, I felt WHY ME? I am a good woman with a good heart, so WHY ME? And WHY do I keep running into these toxic relationships even though I did things a little different this time around. Why can't I get the family I always dreamed of? After crying for over 20 minutes on my porch, I felt like God gave me a rude awakening. It was as if God said to me, "You made your own choices and that's what led you here. Now pick your head up and wipe your eyes!"

I kid you not; it was at that point that I realized my fault in this. I say "fault" as in the fact that we, as people, make our own choices, especially regarding who we date and choose to give our bodies to. We have personal and relationship goals yet, at times, our choices and actions are not leading up to them nor are our choices a reflection of them. The harsh reality I faced about myself was if I wanted marriage before children, why was I having unprotected sex? Why was I giving away my body, especially without a commitment that I was seeking in my heart? Now I wanted to blame him because I made the choice to give him my body countless times. It takes two to get pregnant. Granted he did me wrong and he was deceitful, but it was my choice to date him and have sex. It was a harsh reality that I hadn't had to face before about my choices in dating and the men I gave myself to. To top it off, the fact and harsh reality was that I made the choice to not follow my life and relationships goals.

Accountability:

Because I lived life my way, I felt and thought I was accountable for my actions. From that moment, crying on my porch, I knew I had to do some deep soul searching. How can you blame another for something you willingly made the choice to do? I know many of us as women have given our bodies too many times. We say we want marriage and love yet we move fast in relationships. We have children with men we barely know and we follow our bodies and temporary desires instead of our brains or our core values. We get upset when a man disappoints us yet we usually don't own our part in it for accepting disloyal behavior from men. It's like that old saying goes, "Fool me once, shame on you; fool me twice, shame on me."

That moment on my porch was one of the hardest things I had to deal with about myself. This was not the first time I knew I should have changed how I went about dating, but when you are having a child you must think about this because children are forever. Children tie you to someone regardless of how you feel about that person and regardless if that person lied to you, etc. We can't blame someone else for what we willingly choose to be a part of. Yes, I could say well he lied to me but, in reality, I chose to go against my relationship goals and have unprotected sex. I always say, like the expression goes, "it's a hard pill to swallow!" When you have to acknowledge your choices and their outcomes, you are forced to look deep within you. That's a hard pill to swallow. Not only is it a hard pill to swallow, it takes a lot of time to digest.

The definition of ACCOUNTABILITY: the quality or state of being accountable; *especially*: an obligation or willingness to accept responsibility or to account for one's action (http://www.merriamwebster.com/dictionary/accoun tability). This means that we must have a willingness to accept what the outcome of our choices is. This means we cannot blame others for personal choices we made especially with our bodies. Ask yourself, how can one truly heal if they do not acknowledge any accountability for their own choices?

Healing:

It was not an easy process having to be accountable for my choices. You definitely can't heal if you are busy playing victim. The bad thing about victim feelings is if those feelings stay too long, it will take longer for you to acknowledge your role in the situation, which delays your personal growth. It wasn't easy having to ask myself, "Tanicia what did you truly expect by having unprotected sex?" I also had to ask myself what did I really expect if I chose to have sex even though I claimed I wanted marriage before children. Reality is, even if you use protection, it can fail. If protection fails and you become pregnant, even though you wanted to wait for marriage, how can you blame anyone? As they teach us in middle school, the only 100% guarantee is abstinence.

Even after the day on the porch, it took me almost a year to really understand my accountability. I spent over a year arguing, being pissed off, and being happy for my baby girl. But the biggest thing I spent time on was discovering what about myself I needed to work on. I remember being angry with my daughter's dad and still being disappointed in myself as I settled into being a single mom. During this time, I realized my life was moving slowly due to the mindset I had developed from harboring all these feelings. I had to begin shifting my mindset to start being accountable, to start forgiving, and to start healing so that I could move on. It took two years for me to deal with ME and to finally get tired of being tired. It was hard and I am still a work in progress, as we all are. I had to forgive him to move on but, most importantly, I had to forgive myself first.

You have to deal with the reality that you control your thoughts and your choices, not other people. If you allow others to control your thoughts and harbor grudges, you stop your internal growth. Healing is purely internal but reflected through your external actions. You can't grow without healing and that includes letting go of bad feelings about past choices and acknowledging your choices and their outcomes. You can move past mistakes and move past feeling sorry for yourself. I had to heal myself and stop allowing external things to shape how I felt within. Remember Happiness is a daily choice.

Moving forward:

Everything I discussed is purely internal things that must take place inside of you and your spirit. Change and shift your mindset because it all starts and ends with you. Don't allow harboring bad feelings to stop your personal growth. Learn to forgive and that includes forgiving yourself. One of the things about moving forward is understanding that you must also change some of your past behaviors that possibly caused you to be in that situation or caused you to harbor ill feelings, leaving you stuck. My friend Shannon Brewer said, "Stop allowing negative thoughts to live rent free in your mind, evict them." That means to move forward you must shift your mindset and stop allowing the past to hinder you from moving forward to live a better life. Remember Jesus said, "I have come that they may have life, and that they may have it more abundantly" (John 10:10 New King James Version). Of course, there will be days where you feel up and down but once you make it a point to shift your mindset; your life will slowly change. One of the things I had to realize is that I had to fully understand my self-worth or I would continue to make poor choices in relationships. What does self-worth mean to you? Do you know healing and forgiveness are tied into it?

Self-worth is more than just loving you in relationships. And it's reflected in your actions, especially after you have made mistakes that God wanted you to learn from. Ask yourself, do I know my worth and what does it mean to me? I had to learn that I deserved more. But I would never know what the "more" was if I stayed stuck in the past with past feelings. Through the tough times, I learned I deserved more. God may put us in situations that we will never understand, but we if we have faith and trust Him; things will shift for the better. Keep in mind, that only you control your destiny. What came out of my tears on the porch that day was me realizing my worth. So there was beauty in my dark moment and there can be in yours. Whatever situation you're facing or dealing with, be sure to own your truth in it, learn to cope, and move forward. Once you can learn with every bad situation to be accountable, forgive, and heal, your life will continue to shift to a better place. Remember moving forward requires not looking back and not allowing your past to become your outcome. My theme for 2016 to "Speak Upward, Shift Upward." This means to make it a point, no matter what happens to you or what mistakes you make, to speak positivity over your life. Lastly, remember Accountability then Forgiveness then Healing is where true growth occurs.

Megan Anderson

Age 29

Author-Blogger-Entrepreneur

Website: www.Lipstick-n-sneakers.com

Email: lipstick.n.sneakers@gmail.com

"Dear Daddy"

"Forgiving does not erase the bitter past. A healed memory is not a deleted memory. Instead, forgiving what we cannot forget creates a new way to remember. We change the memory of our past into a hope for our future."

-Beverly Flanigan

March 19, 2015

Dear Daddy,

I don't know if you know who I am, I don't know if you even care. I am Cindy's daughter. I would like the opportunity to get to know why you chose to leave me, why you didn't love me and how you could not care about me.

Megan

I am the child of a single mother. Growing up, I was told that my father never wanted kids so he left us when my mother was 7 months pregnant. She had no choice but to have me because she was too far along to have an abortion. I knew that before I was even born, I was the unwanted, unplanned mistake that my father never cared about. My younger self could never have understood that hearing those words or experiencing those things would affect me as seriously as a grown woman. I didn't realize until I became an adult how this would leave a void; how I was left struggling to find me.

May 7th, 2015

Dear Megan,

I hope this day finds you well, I expected some day that you might reach out and have some questions I will do my best to respond. I am sure your mom has filled you in on what she knows, I will endeavor to fill the gaps. The primary reason I was not involved with you is I was way too immature to raise a child and quite honestly scared to death. Your mother's pregnancy was not planned. I was very clear at the time that I was not interested in kids. I requested a paternity test and the outcome was that beyond a reasonable doubt you were my child. I believed that it was in your best interest if I were not a part of your life, I assumed your mom went on to meet a nice guy, got married and that you had a stable happy childhood. Both of my parents knew about you but respected my privacy as well as your moms. I explained the situation to them just as I explained it to you.

Respectfully...

My mother has been an alcoholic all of my life. She was married and divorced, by the time I was 5 years old, to a man full of broken promises. My step dad was the type of man that would say all of the right things. He would tell me he was "My Dad". He would tell me that he would always be there for me. After their divorce, he would promise to come pick me up. I would lie in the doorway between my room and the hallway glancing, anxiously, through the window at the end of the hall.

Over and over again, I found myself staring at an empty street, waiting for that red Corvette filled with promises that never arrived.

Many years passed until I saw this man again, "My Dad". By this time, I was about thirteen. I was with my mother at the Alameda County Fair and, by chance, we came face-to-face on a walkway near the grass. He seemed excited to see us. He said "Hello" to my mother then looked at me with confusion on his face. "Hello, umm… umm?" I stood there in disbelief, as he stumbled. He couldn't remember my name… Years of abandonment, in the form of sadness, overwhelmed my body, but I could say nothing. I could not tell him he was supposed to be there. I could not show that I still needed to be wanted. I could not explain to him that I needed to understand how a woman is to be treated by a man. I could not let him see that he broke my heart, again…

At thirteen, I knew I was still unwanted. Still unplanned. Still a mistake. But now I was old enough to understand the pain and it felt insurmountable. I cried hard that day.

May 8th, 2015

Dear Daddy,

I do believe that you felt at that time, you not being in my life would be better for me because you were not ready. I have convinced myself over the years, that it had nothing to do with me, and before I arrived, you had your own life and own things going on. My mother got married and divorced, and after their divorce, her ex-husband, who I knew as a father figure, completely stopped all contact. She is now with a man, who I would not consider a father figure, as he didn't treat myself or my mother well.

So, although I've had male figures in my life, I do not consider them to be a father and it is extremely difficult for me to trust. A lot of things recently have prompted this reaching out to you. I have made many bad decisions growing up, in part because I've been looking for someone to fill a void I think every daughter who doesn't have a dad has, at certain points I believed I did not deserve to be loved because my own father did not want me, I now know your decision had nothing to do with me, as hard as it may have been.

Your Daughter...

For years, I struggled to make the right decisions when it came to men. I lost my virginity when I was fourteen and for years after, I continued to let the wrong men into my world. I look back and realize I was searching to be made whole; for someone to love me. Allowing each person to take a piece of me, emotionally, mentally, physically. I felt used. I felt damaged. I felt worthless.

At seventeen, I met a man six years older than me. What I believed to be love at that time was actually lies and manipulation. I didn't know what I deserved and in time, lie returned lie. We had both lied. Deceit returned deceit. We had both cheated. And then, at 27 years old, about a month before our 10-year anniversary, my infidelity and lies forced us both to be honest. About everything. And it was over. The 'us' I knew for 10 years was done. The 'me' I knew, was gone.

Leaving that relationship, I had to now be honest with myself. Be in a relationship with myself. Rediscover myself. And it didn't take long to realize that I didn't actually know who I was, what makes me happy, what I would tolerate, and why I kept making the same mistakes over and over again.

I had learned to mask an extreme lack of confidence and major insecurities. I had learned to question myself. I had learned not to trust any and all men. I had mistaken neglect and poor treatment as love because that's what I knew. I was born into this world, to a hard-working woman who couldn't love herself the way she deserved, choosing alcohol over parenting. And to an absent father who couldn't care less if I was there. Worse, I had blamed myself because I thought I wasn't good enough. I thought I deserved this pain, I expected to be hurt.

June 29, 2015

Megan,

I don't know what is important to you so I don't really know what questions to answer. It is probably as awkward on my end as it is on yours. I am not much of a phone person never have been. So where I see this going in the future is, we both have a level of comfort with one another, which we are developing. And one day if both are agreeable we will meet for coffee. I can understand your curiosity and I don't think it is fair for me to deny you. In closing feel free to drop me an email when you feel like it. Please understand that this is our busy season and it may take a couple of days for me to respond.

Respectfully...

As an adult, I struggled knowing that my father was out there and the decisions I had made were in part because he was not in my life. All the pain I had held inside gave me the desire to reach out to him. I needed to try to understand how a man can leave his only child, regardless of what he thought he originally wanted.

Was he scared? I didn't know how he'd feel. I didn't know how I'd feel talking to him, but I was scared. But I needed to know. So I shed my fear, gathered the courage, and Googled.

There he was, his email address right next to his face. The face that I had only seen in 2 other pictures… Some man, who I do not know, but who is my Daddy…

We've emailed back and forth a few times now. He seems to pick and choose which emails he will respond to. He sent a short email saying that this was the busy season for him and he would try to respond as soon as possible. Those busy days, turned to busy weeks, turned to busy months, with no other emails. The feelings I held onto still weighed heavy on my heart.

Time continued to go by. I'm not sure what made this time different for me but I felt that in order for me to start to heal, I had to let him know. I had to say something.

July 21st, 2015

Dear Daddy,

When writing you I've struggled with things to ask or things to say to you. I've felt like so many parts of me have to be you because even though she raised me, a lot of what my mother does or says is nothing that I would do. I know that as an adult I am my own person but a lot of beliefs come from what you learn from your parents, but, and this is the part that I struggle with, I am not sure where I fit in. As an adult I completely understand your reasons for not being a part of my life and that you've thought I was taken care of. But as the little girl still searching for answers it's so hard to believe that this whole time there was a man out there that missed out on so many important stages. I feel like I've struggled in all ways possible because I never really felt loved from either parent, and although I know I can't change the past I don't want to have false hope for the future. I feel as though I'm pouring my heart out for a man who doesn't even care which is sad because I came from that man. True or not. It's really a weird feeling. There's parts of me that wants to say help me, I need your help.. And then there are the parts that say you can't trust anything about him. I've built up this vision of what I thought you would be like and it's very hard getting away from those thoughts. I'm not even sure if there is anything I need to know or want to know right now. I feel telling you how I've felt is in a way therapy. I don't know what's important for me to know, I don't know what questions I should be asking. I think it's just getting to know you as the man you are today and understanding that person... I think subconsciously I want you to be the one asking me all the things a "dad" is "supposed" to care about, and make sure that if you know you made the wrong decision back then to make sure you make the right ones now, ask me if I need help and follow through, I think I've been looking for you to show me you're not this horrible person who never cared about me. If that's even possible for you to show me, I'm not sure. If that's even how you feel, I'm not sure. Obviously, I'm not to sure of many things right now. What I do know is, I want to know who I am, and that involves learning who you are. I'm extremely guarded and untrusting, I know it may not feel that way seeing that I've been pretty open in regards to my feelings, but I don't want to be hurt by you all over again. You can share whatever info you feel comfortable sharing, because at this point, I don't know anything.

This was over a year ago now… He never responded… I am not exactly sure what I hoped for in getting to know him. But I do know, as a grown woman, him not responding doesn't hurt. I don't feel unwanted, or unplanned, or like the mistake I always thought I was.

I realized me being able to tell him that he hurt me, whether he knew it or not, and that his absence had affected my life, slowly started to heal all those wounds I had. I no longer feel like I need to know why. I no longer feel like I will allow a man to abuse my trust. Not because I don't trust, but because I now know my worth. It's my father who doesn't know his daughter's worth… And that is his loss. Not mine.

February 8th, 2016

Dear Daddy,
I forgive you and wish you nothing but the best.
Megan

I am still on the path to discovering what a broken woman loves. Yes, I say that I am 'broken'. Being broken does not mean that I will be broken forever or that I cannot be mended. I am beautifully broken and I now look at the positive choices I make as the glue that puts the pieces of me back together.

I am beautiful. I am strong. I am independent. In order to be my true self, I had to forgive, not only my parents or my past relationships, but the most important person, myself. I had to dig deep within and truly forgive. I've cried, too many times to count, about the decisions and mistakes I've allowed and made. I understand that there may be chips and cracks in my make-up. I may be wounded and have scar upon scar. I will continue to make mistakes. But those mistakes don't make me. What makes me now is how I choose to rebuild.

Megan Anderson's Bio

Megan Anderson is a 29 year old, single, workaholic who is on a journey to discovering what it means to really be happily broken and starting life over as a single woman.

Growing up in a struggling, single parent home, surrounded by alcoholism, Megan knew she had to grow up and take care of herself at a very young age. She began writing to help take her mind away from the troubled world around her and has started working on her first book, as well as a blog.

Megan has discovered along this self-discovery journey that sharing her life has become therapeutic, she's gone through and overcome many difficult things, made her own mistakes and even though life was hard at times she has had a lot of fun along the way. She believes if a little piece of her story brings something helpful or positive to your life than she has reached one of her goals. She hopes that her story will show that with a little courage and a lot of faith you can change your situation and realize your true worth and the power you hold as a woman.

Follow me on Facebook:

https://www.facebook.com/lipsticknsneakers/

Breaking Through Life's Barriers

Danae Braggs

Age 37

Real Estate Agent, Author, Entrepreneur, Speaker

and all around Superwoman

Pittsburg, CA Native

Business Cell: 925-481-6058

"Closure"

Always having been the strong one, I held myself up to, and beyond, that standard. At least that's what it looked like on the outside. I would describe myself as an egg. A raw egg. Protective hard shell on the outside with a multifaceted inside - the stiff, tough to puncture yoke and the gooey, sticky soft membrane. Let me break it down a bit more. The shell: a hard exterior, tough to break through; protection; the wall. The yoke: the center of my being; where all that I hold dear is stored; where my feelings dwell and are buried deep. This is my core. This is where my value and values are nestled, protected by the wall that is the shell. The membrane is the sticky that bonds me, which connects me to those and what I love. Transparent and dense, it acts as a bridge to my yoke. An outcome that at one point in my life was not guaranteed or even expected. Then I came to a crossroad.

A decision was made for me, an uncomfortable decision that I fought long and hard to keep off the table. I was the epitome of a "good wife". Was. I was the "best mom in the world". Was. In March 2012, that all changed. There was a knock at the door. I walked over and pulled it open. There stood a tall gentleman clutching a manila envelope. A familiar face with a calm voice. I looked past him. It was a beautiful sunny, what I call sprinter (spring/winter), day. Seconds before the knock, I had just finished the phone call that I thought was the biggest change in my life. I enrolled in, and paid for, my real estate courses. Then the knock. I opened the door. I looked down at his hand and noticed the envelope he was holding. He immediately extended his arm to hand me the envelope and said, "I had nothing to do with this." My husband, who at this point lived around the corner from us, the one whose idea it was to separate to work on ourselves individually, the one who said we'll come back together even stronger, the one who I had just gone on a date with a few days before, had filed for divorce. The person who infiltrated my wall, waded through my membrane and penetrated my yolk, had just turned my world upside down.

In the midst of my life falling apart I found two peaceful moments where my mind was clear enough to say two peaceful but very specific prayers. Initially, one had nothing to do with the other and were said at separate times, but later God showed me that they had everything to do with each other. It was like He was sitting on the edge of his seat waiting for me to say the exact words to make this specific step to really push this phase into motion. The phase of closure. The closure I was fighting so hard to prevent. I had unknowingly prayed a block right onto the path of my crusade to put my family back together. My plight to eliminate this looming closure just took a turn for the worse.

The first prayer was simple. I asked God to show me who was for me and who wasn't. It was almost like there was an immediate universal shift that happened that I could physically feel. Like I was blind and my vision had been restored the moment I said "Amen." From that moment on, I saw people around me in their truest form. Perhaps it was because from the time I was very young, I realized my true gift of discernment. I have always been able to tell who people really were and have always read energy well. At some point in my life this gift was definitely clouded by a lot of things that I put under one large umbrella of distraction. In order to sharpen a skill, or perfect a craft, one needs clarity. At this point I realized that clarity was what I had been missing for the past 14 plus years. In the midst of my life falling apart, God gave me clarity.

Secondly, I said a prayer and asked God for all the things I wanted/needed my husband to be. As specific as the prayer was I never mentioned his name and I didn't realize it until two years later when we separated again. Yeah, we reconciled (or so I thought) and dismissed the divorce. In the time leading up to the second separation, my husband never lived up to any of these specific traits that I prayed for. To be honest, it wasn't until we were separated again and I knew it was really over that I even remembered this prayer. It hit me like a ton of bricks one day as I was talking with a friend. I started noticing some of the specific things in my friend that I asked God to pour into my husband. But how could this be? He was just a really good friend. I fought it off. No, I'm having fun and enjoying being single. It couldn't be real... but it was. My mind was clear enough to see what God was trying to show me. This friend met the requirements; he had all the pre-qualifying criteria. Everything I asked God for, He showed me in this friend. Then I realized that one specific detail was left out. His name. I prayed this elaborately specific prayer about what I wanted/needed my husband to be and I failed to mention his name. The darkness had been lightened. My mind was no longer clouded by the transference of negative energy, secrets and the "what ifs" of failure. Once I let go, God blessed me with everything that I asked for and then some. He blessed me with someone who I wanted and who wanted to infiltrate my wall, wade through the membrane and completely penetrate my yolk. Closure.

Four years later and the journey toward wholeness is in full gear. Eliminating negativity as much as possible since that pivotal point of no return has allowed me to extend my new found clarity. My mind has been elevated and everything my negative situation made me not want, I want again. All the things that were taken away have been, and are being, replaced. I no longer feel like I'm wasting time. My light is definitely shining and I am now completely walking in my purpose.

Danae Braggs Bio:

A Pittsburg, CA native, Danae Braggs is an all-around SUPER WOMAN. Becoming a mother at 16, she had every reason to also become a statistic. She never did. She soared above the odds and surpassed a lot of lack luster expectations. Today she is a successful entrepreneur, real estate agent, and author; just to name a few of her many accomplishments. Her philanthropic endeavors almost always promote her beloved city, Pittsburg. She has been quoted as saying "I'm from here from here..." An advocate for children, housing rights, self-sufficiency and more, Danae shows and proves that she is the epitome of the term SUPER WOMAN.

I am not a VICTIM, I am a VICTOR

Philicia Jones

Age 38

Antioch, Ca.

Author-Plus Size Model- Veteran- Role Model

Facebook-Philicia Jones   Instagram-Simplysexxy124

Business email: Philicia.jones124@gmail.com

"Unhinged"

In the beginning, I remember an awesome childhood. I remember playing outside with the other kids and spending time with my mom and my sister. I grew up in the projects until I was about two years old, but then we moved to a better part of San Francisco. We moved to the Fillmore District because my mother got a better job, which was great. Our lives were finally getting better until my mom met a man at the bus stop. I thought it was a good thing because my mom was happy for a while, until I told her that he asked me to jack him off one day. I remember like it was yesterday.

I was about six years old at home with him alone. I heard him coming down the hallway to the living room where I was watching cartoons. When he came around the corner, he had on nothing but a red t-shirt and socks, with his private out. I couldn't believe what I was looking at. You just walk into the kitchen like nothing was wrong? His private was hanging out and I was completely confused about what I was seeing. My mom always told me and my sister to stay away from people like him, but he was living in our home. As he walked past me down the hallway to my mom's bedroom I heard him call my name, "Lee-lee come in here." I was terrified, but I was always told to listen to my elders. So I went down the long dark hall. That day it was the longest hallway ever! When I got to the bedroom, he was lying on my mom's bed naked. I stopped at the door and dropped my head in disgust and terror. He said, "Come here to the edge of the bed." So I did, and he asked me to help him put lotion on because he just gotten out of the shower. He made me use my mom's Lubriderm lotion on his hairy chest. I was disgusted and terrified at the same time. As I was rubbing lotion on him, he started to rub on his private parts, which was creepy and scary. He grabbed my little hands and wrapped them around his private and started moving my little hands up and down. Some white stuff came out, but he just wiped it off and kept going. I wanted to run and hide, but he was holding my hands too tightly. I couldn't stand the sight, the smell, or what was going on. I was just praying that it would all be over soon. All I could think about was telling my mom and how she would make him leave and protect me.

As I was walking away he said to me, "Don't tell anyone. This is our little secret." When he said that I was confused because my mom always told me that if someone does anything to me that was inappropriate to tell her. So I was scared to tell my mom right away, so I waited a week. We both were in the kitchen cooking. I can still smell the chicken frying. As my mom was making my plate, I said, "Mom I have something to tell you." She said, "Okay, tell me." I told her that her boyfriend was walking around the house with nothing on, just a red t-shirt and tube socks. Then I told her that he made me touch him. My mom paused for a second, then she put my plate on the table and told me to eat. She told me she would be right back. I was waiting to hear a lot of screaming and yelling but all I heard was silence. Then I heard my mom call my name, "Lee-lee come here!" I had to walk down that long dark hallway again. I stopped at the door. He was on the side of the bed throwing up because he was coming down off of a crack high. He lifted his head with vomit hanging from his lip. As he wiped it away he said, "Your mom told me you told her I let you touch me." I said, "Yes I did." He said, "I don't remember that. And if I did, it won't happen again." The room reeked of vomit and my mom never looked away from the TV. I felt so alone at that moment. And that wouldn't be the last time my mom let me down.

I felt alone in our home as I grew up. I had a few suicide attempts because I didn't get any counseling for the molestation or the depression I had as kid. Ever since I was a child, I have been dealing with the sexual abuse. And as an adult, it really affected me in my relationship with men, my mom, and my sister. I was overly sexual as a teenager, which led me to becoming pregnant at 13 years old. I was drinking and smoking weed. It took me a few years to come to my senses and get my GED.

I joined the Navy to make my life better for my son. But what I didn't know was that what I went through as a child was only the beginning. From the day I joined the Navy, I was harassed by men. I did not know that I was in a man's Navy and it was a free-for-all on women. It was so bad that, I, as a woman, who was abused as a child, who had grown strong enough to report their abuse, was told by the people in the military to keep it a secret or be kicked out of the Navy. So I had to keep all the sexual abuse to myself and just take it for 15 years. Eventually, I said I couldn't take it anymore. I got out of the Navy without retiring. It was also hard to deal with the women in the Navy who were insecure about my beauty. The women would think I slept around because I was friendly and men and women loved me like I loved everyone else. Women were so worried about me stealing their men that they never got the opportunity to know a good friend. I'm at a point in my life where I'm successful in my career with over of 18 years of federal service. I own three cars and a house I now have three awesome children and a granddaughter who's four.

I'm a work in progress and I still have a long way to go, but I have a great man by my side who loves me for me and who completes me. I'm his wife and his best friend. I want people to understand that whatever you go through in life to be strong through the situation. And if you can make it through, you're a victor and not still a victim. To my military personnel, don't let anyone, not even your superiors, tell you not to report any abuse. Even if it's verbal, it all hurts the same in the end. Love yourself first and foremost because no one can love you like you can. Stay tuned for my upcoming book to find out what happened in between all my madness. I will have you laughing on one page and crying on the next and cheering for me by the end.

Philicia Jones Bio:

Philicia Jones is the mother of three beautiful awesome children Philicia has overcome childhood molestation by her mother's boyfriend who soon after became her mother's husband. She later became a teen mom at the age of 13. She never let things hold her back and she went on to get her GED and joined the Navy in 1997 to begin her career as a military woman. Philicia was faced with many obstacles and mental anguish in her life. She went on to become a plus-size model and is currently enrolled in school to get her bachelor's degree in financial management. Philicia experienced being molested and raped, becoming a young mother, being homeless, attempting suicide on many occasions, yet she is still here - dealing with her past and looking forward to her future. She's a strong, loving, and caring woman and lives for her children. She has learned in order to remain a good mom she has to put herself first in life. Philicia is ready for the journey that lies ahead of her. And by sharing her story, she hopes to give young ladies and older women the courage to come and voice their story and not hide. And if you have mental issues, she encourages you to talk about them to your children and to your family. Be involved and get better.

Keisha Frowner

Age 39

Author-Educator-Mother

Klaugh983@yahoo.com

Thank you Carol for your support. Just Start! Keisha Frowner

"A Living Witness"

Growing up, I always wanted my dad around. I was told that he and my mom separated when I was two, when my mom and I moved from L.A to Oakland. My dad was not there for me after the move and I don't really remember him at that young age. When I would get upset at my mom I would let her know that I wanted to stay with my dad. That's when my mom would respond back and make comments about my father that a child should not hear. When I was four, I remember going back to L.A with my mom on a Greyhound bus to visit her boyfriend's side of the family. My mom had a son by him and we stayed down there for about a week. That's when I got molested by my mom's boyfriend. This had an effect on me as a child. In the first grade, I would get notes sent home because of my behavior at school. Back then you had to bring your note back to school with a parent's signature. When I turned sixteen, I started having boyfriends because my mom told me this was the age I could start dating. I always wanted to be with someone who would show me affection by holding hands in public and just giving me the attention I was seeking. Growing up in the streets of Oakland was not a joke. There was a lot of drug activity in my neighborhood and some of the girls I went to school with had boyfriends that were drug dealers. It was by the grace of God that I graduated from high school without having sex and getting pregnant. I was raised in a single parent home, where my mom raised me and two other siblings. People in my neighborhood knew me as the church girl and a basketball player. So when I became pregnant with my first child, I was the talk of the town in the beauty salon, the church, and in the streets. It caught them by surprise by me having a child out of wedlock and not been married.

I met my kid's father, who I will call J.P., after my first year in college in the summer of '96 in Oakland. He seemed to be a gentleman and was well dressed. I was not attracted to him, but gave him my number. I was working at Burger King so my focus was not on dating. That summer I do remember handling my business. We soon got together and he took me to his place where he cooked me breakfast. Prior to this, he did tell me that he only had two daughters from a previous relationship and spoke well of them. He talked about how smart they were. I noticed in the apartment there was a kid's bedroom. He claimed that it was his sister's kids' room. This was a red flag that I did not realize at the time. That is why it is so important to ask questions and get to know someone before you get into a relationship. There were other red flags, such as his pager going off and him going out alone to answer when we were on our date. I remember telling one of his relatives how nice of a man he was and she just smiled at me.

J.P. was pushing marriage too fast. We had not even known each other that well. We were engaged after about two and a half months. I felt like he was sensitive to a woman's need and all he wanted was me, but I was about to find out the truth about this man through trials, tribulations, and life lessons. He would buy me clothes and say the things I wanted to hear. I went back to college in Fresno County to play my second year of basketball at a community college. Around fall time, J.P. came to visit me. After the second visit, we started having sex. That's when I started seeing the real person he was. His tone and attitude changed towards me. I compromised and gave in because of fear. I wanted to be married before having sex. This is what I heard preached in the church and I had made a decision in my teenage years to wait. J.P. would call me names and not return my phone calls when I called him. One day in basketball practice, I was feeling more tired than usual. I was not getting up and down the court like I normally did. I decided to go to the doctor and I remember the nurse coming out of the office telling me the news that I was pregnant. When I told J.P. he asked me what I wanted to do. I told him that I was going to keep the baby. He seemed like he did not care. I thought he was a good father because of how well he spoke about his daughters, but I had not even met J.P.'s children and to find out if he was a responsible father.

I had to go back to Oakland to live with my mom. I felt hopeless and wondered what people would say about me. I was engaged, but that does not mean anything if you are not married. There was no support from him and I was alone dealing with my pregnancy. He would come by when it was convenient for him to just have sex and then he would leave. Occasionally we would go out on a date and when I would bring up marriage he did not want to discuss it. I still stayed with him because I felt stuck in this situation and being pregnant. I would call him and he would not respond, leaving me hanging. I had my first child and after about six months I had to move out of my mom's house. I had to move out because of a disagreement with my mom. I faced homelessness with nowhere to go with my child. I walked down the street to a relative's house and stayed the night. The next morning J.P. came and took the baby and me to a random person's house that I did not know while he lived somewhere else. We stayed at this person's house for about three months and then I had to leave. This was somebody else's house I was staying in and I understood. I went from shelter to shelter. While I was there in those shelters, I was determined to get back on my feet and to find a job to take care of my daughter, in spite of what I was going through. I had finally decided to get on welfare to take care of my daughter's needs. One night when I was pregnant with my first child, J.P. drove me to a vacant parking lot and said that he would do something to me. I was afraid to say anything about how I was being treated and I did not have a support system that I could confide in. I found placement in transitional housing in Oakland near Telegraph Ave. It was during this time that I found out I was pregnant with my second child. I was abused physically, financially, and emotionally by this man. I stayed with him because of fear. I was afraid that he would harm me if I left. I found out he had other children, more than the two he had by other women. He did not tell me the truth about his age; he was 10 years older than me. When we first met I was 20 and J.P. told me that he was 24 years old. He was cheating on me with other women. People seemed to know all his business except me. And word was out that he was already married to someone. J.P. was not telling me the truth about who he was. How could I get myself out of this mess when I felt like I gave my all to this man? He also had alias names that he used. My first child stayed with her aunt on their dad's side around the time I moved in the transitional housing, and then my second daughter, six weeks after being born. To me, I felt like an unfit mother because he would not check on his children regularly or provide for them like he was supposed too. I made sure I checked on my children when the aunt had them, but felt bad because of my situation and for not being there for them like I should. I wanted to be responsible for my own children and not have anyone raise them for me. I would get the girls almost every weekend. At the time I was working and going to Merritt College during the spring of '99.

Enough was enough from this man. In May of '99, J.P. got very upset with me because he wanted the money that I had worked for from my job. On this day I spoke up and stood up for myself. I told him how I felt about the relationship and he threatened to harm me. I remember being upstairs and getting off the phone with J.P. and I heard a still small voice say, "Leave." When it says God will make a way of escape, I am a living witness. I was calling different places. The first place I called was Nevada State and they were willing to take me in at a domestic violence shelter. They were asking me a lot of questions, trying to make sure that I was safe. Then I called a San Francisco shelter and they asked me the same thing. I had both of my children with me on that day, which was a blessing. Their aunt had gone out of town. I could now be a responsible parent. He kept paging and calling me, asking me to bring the children outside to him. I refused and he called the police on me. A female police officer came and looked into the situation. She told me that J.P. seemed like a con artist. She said that he would have to go to court to see his children. The next day I had to get a restraining order against him. I had someone go with me to get it. She was just as nervous as I was. I moved to a domestic violence shelter in San Francisco. During this time of leaving, I was scared of J.P. finding out where I was and harming me. I was afraid of the unknown and did not know how things would turn out by leaving. There were other women at the shelter who had been in abusive relationships and I was not alone. I stayed there for three months and then moved to Concord transitional housing for domestic violence, where I stayed for two years. It is now called STAND, formally known as Battered Women's Alternatives (BWA).

During this time I went back to college for Early Childhood Development and got my AA degree. The staff at the transitional housing educated the women about domestic violence awareness. This is where I learned about recognizing the red flags in an abusive relationship. The women that stayed there would share their stories of what they went through. I would go to support group meetings once a week and I also received counseling. After my two years of stay at STAND, I went to another transitional housing program for a year in Antioch, California, with my two girls and got a job as a preschool teacher. I moved into my own place for the first time. It was not easy finding housing for me and my two daughters. About two years later, the county caught up with J.P. and I got papers in the mail about going to court for child support. I did not want to go by myself, so I asked my sister to go with me. When she told me that she could not go with me, I realized that I could no longer run and hide from him. I still had to be aware of my surroundings, but got tired of constantly living in fear. I went to court and soon started to receive child support. As of now my oldest daughter, Lorenna, is finishing up her first year in college. She is the first to attend a four-year college in our immediate family, but will not be the last. My other daughter, Charlene, will be graduating from high school in June 2016 and is very talented with music and basketball. Their father has not been in their lives and that was a choice that he made. This is not what I wanted, but I had to do what was best for my children. Yes, I am a living witness. I refused to be a victim no matter how long it took to get on my feet. You too can persevere and not let your circumstances hold you back. Leaving was not easy and yes, I was afraid, but God gave me the courage to do it. I told myself that I would not play house with men and would set this standard for my daughters. God is not through working on me. There is a new chapter of my life being written. My book will be coming out in the spring of 2017. Life is a journey and every day is an opportunity to overcome and better yourself.

Keisha Frowner Bio:

Keisha Frowner was born in Los Angeles, CA, and raised in Oakland, CA. She is the first born of her siblings and a single mother of two beautiful daughters, Lorenna and Charlene. Keisha is currently a preschool teacher and finds joy in making a difference in a child's life. Growing up in Oakland, she was exposed to seeing drug dealings and gang activity within her neighborhood. Going to church and playing basketball helped Keisha stay focused and at a young age she learned the importance of having a good work ethic. Keisha graduated from Fremont High School in Oakland, CA, and went on to attend a community college. After being in college for a year and a half, Keisha found out that she was pregnant and was forced to leave school to take care of her child. After having both of her children, Keisha went back to school and received her A.A. degree. She graduated from Diablo Valley College, where she studied Early Childhood Development. Although

Keisha suffered an abusive relationship and lived in transitional housing, she was able to persevere and create a better life for her and her family. Keisha wants to inspire other women to never let go of their dreams and to finish what they start.

Kanishia Wallace

Age 34

ENTREPRENEUR | MENTOR | AUTHOR

Unique Living Project

Health. Happiness. Freedom.

For Project Details:

Text 'EZRFN13820' to 313131

Sacramento, CA

"Think Like A Winner: Mind Your Mindset"

Have you ever felt like life in general was totally against you? Had a bad start to life? Maybe even wish you could rewrite an entire chapter of your life? Well, you're not alone. Many people, including myself, have felt the same way. We've all experienced negative things in our lives at some point, but its how one chooses to deal with the objectives that really matter. Often, life can throw curve balls when you least expect them. It is our God given right to choose our mindset, positive or negative, before the day even begins. Personally, I've witnessed where many people who've been mistreated, have come from terrible backgrounds, have been homeless, even struggled with depression, physically broken and even financially sick, yet still they've managed to live their lives as a victor! Whereas, on the other hand, others have allowed their circumstances to dictate their future in negative ways. Usually, it's not the circumstance that impacts the most; it's the attitude toward the outcome that truly defines the person.

According to Merriam-Webster's dictionary, a *victim* is one that is subjected to oppression, hardship, or mistreatment and a *victor* is a person who defeats an enemy or opponent in battle and is seen as a winner, champion and a conqueror. Victors tend to take responsibility of a situation, looking ahead with optimism and hope, and they accept their need to grow before moving on. While victims look for others to blame. Victims usually have no hope or dreams for the future. Victors, on the other hand, usually plan for theirs. The fact is, life has its way of happening to us. The real question is, how can you change your negative thoughts to think like a winner when it comes to life?

Rescued At a Young Age

I, like many adults today, struggled with a victim mentality that took root in my early childhood years. No one gave me a manual on how to cope with life's situations, so I had to learn on my own. As a little girl, I didn't have a very close relationship with my biological father, but years later we've been able to develop a strong bond that's unconditional. Thankfully, I now know, love, and adore my father for our many reasons. One reason in particular is because despite his attempts to connect with me, his love never failed over the years. For as long as I could remember, my mom would always encourage me to build a solid relationship with my father and to this day I'm glad she did. Nothing could've prepared me for the life I had ahead. The mental obstacles I would endure would change my life forever. With limited understanding of how life and death worked as a child, I found myself surrounded by death at an early age.

Before I knew it, I'd lost six very important people, all just a few years apart. Here is where the world I knew collapsed! It all began the morning my mother, Wanda, had a ruptured brain aneurysm, the 'ballooning out' of a weak spot in the wall of a brain artery. Unfortunately, in one day, it seemed like our lives changed forever. I was only nine years old at the time of her death. My mother was all I knew. I was so confused and angry with God! How could this happen to someone so important to me? I was devastated, torn, and broken hearted! Without warning my babysitter, Dorothy, who practically helped raise me, passed away not too long after my mother. No one could prepare me for these losses! Shortly after Dorothy was called home to heaven, my grandmother, my mother's mother Dora, took me in to live with her. I smile about it now, but back then I cried and complained because I thought my grandmother was so mean! I realize she loved tough because she knew life could be tougher.

At the time, I was the only child who lived with my grandmother. As if we hadn't suffered enough loss, my grandmother Dora suddenly passed away. I really felt helpless. A few years after her passing, one of my favorite uncles, Scottie (uncle Ram) passed away, too. As if I wasn't traumatized enough, Paul, my stepfather, who loved me like his own, had a heart attack and never recovered. So much death surrounding me at a young age created a very angry, bitter, sad little girl inside me. At this point, I learned that we have no control over who lives or dies. The fact of the matter is, those who are born will die, some faster than others. For now, the best thing to do is love one another as long as possible! As I look back, God has been my saving grace the entire way.

At what seemed like my lowest moments, God sent his angels to cover me every day. One in particular, I called her Granny, Mrs. Barber, was a friend of our family who loved me. She welcomed me into her home to stay. At this time, I was only eleven years old. Gratefully, at Granny's I had other kids to play with and a permanent place to call home. Up until this point, life had left me weak and afraid for my future, but deep inside I still had hope. Before I knew it, many summers and winters had come and gone. Thank God for Granny who stood in the place of my mother for many years before going to heaven herself! Death is never something we look forward to, but it is a part of living. These are obstacles in life that are designed to make us stronger.

"Strength does not come from winning. Your struggles develop your strength. When you go through hardships and decide not to surrender, that is strength."

- Gandhi

A Greater Plan by Design

God is often blamed for the negative things that happen to us and is usually given less praise for the good things in our lives. Fortunately, God is the Beginner and the Finisher. In every situation, good or bad, there is a message to be learned. Technically, everything that happens to us is a direct reflection on how we interpret things. If we believe everything in life is against us, usually that's what we manifest into existence. We have no control over certain things in life, but we do have the ability to choose how we deal with every situation. Do we bask in the pity of life or do we hope and believe for the best in everything?

Emotionally, I was run down. I began to seek the attention of boys (you can only imagine) and ditch school to hangout. I felt there was a void in my heart. I constantly tried to fill the void by seeking love and attention in all the wrong places. Nothing I did seemed to fill this heavy void. Until I remembered the Bible verses grandma Dora shared with me. I began to pray faithfully. When things felt the most out of control, I found peace in the first scriptures I learned. The first was the Lord's Prayer after my mother passed. At night, I would cry myself to sleep after reciting Matthew 6:9 *Our Father in heaven...* It never failed, when I felt the most unwanted or hate in my heart I would turn to 1 John 4:4, *Little children, you belong to God and have overcome them, because He who is in you is greater than he who is in the world.* I learned to trust God to fill me up with His Spirit of forgiveness and comfort. I noticed things began to change when I allowed God to work through my negative thoughts, spirit of blame, and depression. More so now, I understand allowing God to fight for me and giving Him complete control over my life gives me strength and courage to face all circumstance even when I'm most afraid.

Adapt a Survivor Mentality

There is something about enduring pain and going through changes in life that can bring a sense of victory and strength. It is important to understand, that no one is exempt from misfortunes. We all fall victim from time to time when situations present themselves and in order to regain control we have to decide to change our negative attitude immediately. First, it's an intentional thought process not to allow negativity to rule over our lives. Be reminded not to give power to blame. Don't be so quick to point the finger at God or Satan for the decisions we make or the misfortunes we have no control over. Someone once told me, find a way to be a part of the solution rather than adding to our problems. For a while, I held a victim mentality that kept me from my full potential. Once I recognized how to deal with my negative mentality, a huge weight was lifted and I found another reason to live!

At an early age, I began to build a relationship with God. I had no idea what the future held for me but I knew God had a plan that was bigger than just me. God became my center and the One I relied on daily. Good and bad days all grew better because I started to recognize the good aspects, in even the bad days. I was reminded through prayer to shut down the negative self-talk. Not until I reached my adult years did I realize I'd never received official grief counseling as a kid after the loss of my loved ones. This plays a big part in the healing process. Looking back, I still remember my fourth grade teacher, Mrs. Tower, being the only one to sit me down and ask me how my mother's passing made me feel. I remembered saying that she (my mother) left me, over and over again! I didn't know then that God had already had His plan in place for their lives and mine. Reminded by God's favor over my life, I've been able to regain control and use it to move me forward mentally & spiritually.

Now I understand, I have a greater assignment placed over my life. I'm on a personal mission to reach and inspire others who may need support just like I did. For all who may feel abandoned, angered, lost, mistreated, afraid that life will continue its mission of misfortune, I'm here to share that there is good news and hope for them. When we learn to mind our mindsets, love from the inside will pour outward; that's when life becomes easier and a little more forgiving and enjoyable at best. As a child, I struggled internally, but now I'm sure I've adapted a survivor mentality by simply managing my thoughts!

Attitudes & Outcomes

Every test in our lives either makes us bitter or makes us better! It's easier to become a victim to the circumstances that happen around you. But the champion inside us all still has a chance to make our future lives greater by changing our attitudes. We have to take responsibility and find the good in every situation. Usually, circumstances will remain the same no matter what, good or bad. So take full control over how you think and feel about everything on a daily basis. Life can be harsh if you allow it to be that way towards you. I've learned to be bigger than the obstacles that cross my path. Don't allow the minor things in life to have a greater impact than necessary; it's easy to fall victim if you're not conscious of how you're feeling. Your attitude determines your altitude in life. I remember reading a book called, *The Battle Field of the Mind*, by Joyce Meyers.

It focuses on winning the battle between good and evil thoughts in the mind by implementing biblical principles into our daily lives. Our mind is the ultimate battlefield where there is spiritual warfare between our thoughts. Learning to intentionally control our thoughts and attitudes will drastically change our lives for the better. Thank God now for your new positive outlook on life.

It's not impossible to be positive about everything! It does take prayer, faith, and action (see *Matthew 21:22)*. Step back and evaluate your life to see that it's all worth fighting for. As a little girl, in a world of unfairness, disbelief, grief, sadness and anger, it took my childhood experiences for me to process that there is *purpose* for the *pain* and loss I endured. As a young adult, I learned not to focus on the pain, but to have a new perspective even over the things I had no control over. I learned to choose my reactions especially when others looked to get a reaction. Pain is there to promote change and growth in all of us. One of my mentors once told me not to just *go through it* (the mess) but to *grow through it*. Sadly, many told me that I would be less than what I've become today. I've shown every doubter. To deal with the world at times we have to put on our blinders and be deaf to negativity, dream snatchers, and naysayers. Why? Because negativity is everywhere! My life took a turn for the greater good when I decided to stop settling and living my life through the lens of others. Make up your mind to be free from others' opinions of you and make the shift without anyone's permission. Allow yourself to grow through the difficult times. Don't just settle for a "barely get by" life. Reach for greatness within because you decide to make a difference!

Although our days on earth are numbered, we are called to be greater. At the age of 41 years old, my mother was called to heaven. When she left this world, she took most of her dreams and aspirations to the grave. For many years, her death was a fear I allowed life to cripple me. Instead of being motivated to chase my goals and dreams, I worried about my future. Getting clear on my vision and purpose has created a warrior spirit inside me that can't be broken. Now that I realize I have more to achieve in this lifetime I'm full steam ahead. I have three amazing children and a husband who truly loves me and I adore them! To this day, they're my biggest supporters. Truly, I am the example I want my children to learn from, therefore I have to grow myself daily. Our motto is, if our dreams don't scare us, then we're not dreaming big enough! This is our way to hold ourselves accountable and mind our mindset daily!

Understand, where you land in life isn't where you have to stay! Ask yourself often, am I living up to my true potential? What can I do now to change my circumstances? How can I allow God to use even the bad situations for good? Find ways to turn old mess into a new message that can be shared with the world. Our days on earth are numbered, so don't live with regret or wish you could have done something different in your lifetime. Take pride in building your dreams and goals today versus taking them with you in your final days. Spend more time in prayer and reflect on the things you want out of life according to His word. Even as a little girl, I was determined to survive my losses! Stand in your faith and trust that the plan is greater than your current situation. Even though life has the ability to break spirits, use the pain and frustrations to fuel the positive change you want to see happen. Despite your past and/or current circumstances, you have the capability to re-write a new beginning today. Don't be afraid to start where you are; be grateful for what makes us stronger. And remember, God is the *Creator* who allows us to be the designers that design the lives we want to live!

Kanishia Wallace Bio:

Kanishia Wallace is a God loving Christian believer, a humble wife, a proud mother of three, a business owner, a natural born entrepreneur, a student and a leader in the community. She is an innovative thinker, a mentor and a steward who's on a relentless pursuit of purpose. Kanishia Wallace was born and raised in Fresno, CA. She knew at an early age that she had a reason to live and always knew she had been born to help others get what they need in life as well. She always knew her purpose was to be greater. Kanishia left Fresno after high school in 1999, and began the Criminal Justice program at California State University, Sacramento, where she earned a Bachelor of Science degree a few years later. She is one of the few in her family to go on and complete a four year college degree because of the dreams and goals she wanted to accomplish; however, God's plan for her life was different. The spirit of entrepreneurship was unleashed as she had a desire to be her own boss. In 2008, Kanishia launched her networking group *BoldBeautifulWomen Empowered*. In 2013, she launched *Unique Living,* a health & nutrition business. Kanishia considers herself a jack of many trades, but her true passion is to inspire others to get what they need in life to be successful. Her mission is to dream achieve, to live a life of more than enough and never in lack, and to leave a legacy for generations that her children's children will be proud of. Her name is Kanishia Wallace and she thrives on the success of others!

How I turned my MESS into a MESSage

Sharice Porter

Age 43

Hayward, CA

Co-founder of InPowerment University

shariceporter1@gmail.com

"Please be patient God isn't finished with me yet"

As I look back over my life I cannot believe I have made it this far. There were many times I wanted to give up. My friends told me time and time again that they would not have been able to endure what I had been through. I realized late in life that it was not me, but the great I AM that was working behind the scenes for my good. I will tell you more about HIM later. First let's get into my story. I came into this world two months early on a rainy weekend in December. My parents thought they had more time. I came on into this world kicking and screaming none-the-less as my mom's "ladybug" and my dad's "baby girl." They had lost their first daughter five years earlier to SIDS. Although that tragic loss was hard on my parents, they were determined to have a family. My older brother was born three years after my sister, Seana Denise. As a young child my mind was full of wonder and hope for my future. I wanted to have my hands in everything. Some of my earliest memories were spent at Charles Drew Elementary school in San Francisco, CA. I enjoyed learning and helping others do their best. My weekends were spent with my family. Saturday mornings started with cartoons, breakfast and Soul Train. My parents caught on to my dancing ability while watching me catch on to the latest moves that I saw on

73

television. So my mom enrolled me into dance class. By this time my family had moved to San Jose with hopes of better jobs and a better life. My mom started working at Lockheed in Santa Clara, while my dad drove the buses for Muni in San Francisco. My brother and I became latchkey kids since our parents worked during the day. I thought I had it all. You know the life that we all dream about.....nice home, nice cars, family vacations and activities? Life was great or so I thought....until one sad morning in October my mother woke me and my brother up to get us ready for school like she always did. She would say, "Rise and shine!" That morning she complained that she did not feel well. My brother and I urged her to stay home for our own selfish reasons. She assured us that she would be fine and she drove us to our Grandparents' house, which was our drop off and pick up point during the school year, since my parents did not want us to be latchkey children. As my mother walked back to the car, my brother and I urged her once again to stay home and allow us to stay home as well, to care for her. She smiled with pain behind her smile and confirmed that she would be fine and she would see us later that day . . . well I guess I could say she lied to us that day . . . things as we knew them would never be the same.

Two o'clock on the dot the bell rang. Time to go home! Thank goodness! I was eight years old and in the 5th grade. I found my cousins and we started our walk home. As we turned the last corner before reaching my Grandparents' house, I could see my mom's red Toyota Corolla in the distance! I got excited and took off leaving my cousins to eat my dust. As I made my way to the house, I saw lots of my family members outside. I bypassed them and opened the screen door and ran inside. They didn't matter; I was on the search to find my mommy! I made my way into the dining room of my Grandparents' house. I called out for my mom, no response. As I walked to the bathroom a white plastic bag caught my eye with the words "patient's belongings" on it. I couldn't help but look inside. Inside the bag were my mother's clothes that I knew she had on that morning. What? Why are my mom's clothes in a bag? Where is she? I rushed back outside to find my brother in tears and my cousins holding him. I asked him, "Where is mommy?" Just then, a car drove up and my father got out of the car. Wait, he is supposed to be in San Francisco . . . I knew something was wrong.

My dad told me and my brother to grab our things, he was taking us home. The ride home was dreadful. Dead silence. I had so many questions bubbling inside of me, but I knew to keep my mouth shut until we made it home. We were in my mom's car, the red Toyota. I was just with her hours earlier in this car. I imagined her on the road driving to work. Did she pull over? Did she make it into her work building? What happened to her? When is she coming home? I want my mommy!!! We pulled into the driveway of our home, the place where I felt safest, 527 Glenburry Way. This time I didn't feel safe at all. My father asked us to go get dressed for bed and then come back down so we could talk.

I climbed into his lap and laid my head on his chest. My brother sat in a chair next to him. My father began, "Mommy had a stroke. She is very sick. She is in the hospital and she is going to be there for a while." Before the last word came out of his mouth I began to cry. My questions started, "What is a stroke? When is she coming home? How did this happen? Daddy!!!" He said, "I don't know, I don't know and I don't know." The fact that he didn't answer my questions made me angry. I didn't think about the fact that he too was hurting inside. At that point, all that mattered was I was hurt, angry and afraid. I jumped out of his lap and ran upstairs to my room where I cried myself to sleep.

The next morning he woke me up and told me to get dressed. We were going to see Mommy. I got dressed and met my brother at the front door. We were ready. We didn't say much to each other, but our eyes told the story. We had to get to our Mommy and see what was really going on. Daddy took us to McDonald's on the way to the hospital. I loved McDonald's, but my stomach was so tied in knots I couldn't enjoy my pancakes and sausage breakfast. It was a long drive to the hospital. We drove from San Jose to Redwood City. There was a lot of time for my brain to think about what Mommy was going to look like. My young imagination was not able to give me the picture of what I was about to see.

We made it to the hospital and when the elevator doors opened I saw my grandmother and my mother's two sisters. We waited in this large corridor for what seemed like forever while my dad went to speak with the doctors. He came back and said they are bringing her out now. I was excited until I saw the gurney roll down the corridor. The person on the gurney was pale, with a shaved head that had a dent in one side of it, and tubes coming out of her nose and arm. My aunt said, "There's your mommy!" I defiantly said, "No it's not!" I was in shock. Did anybody care? This is not my mom! Where is her hair? Why is she so pale? My aunt grabbed my arm and said, "Say hi to your mommy!" I said hi quickly and ran back to my seat. I started to cry. There I was with my brother staring at this body they say is our mom. All I could think was, "Does anybody care about us?"

After the shock of viewing the person in the hospital bed "they" said was my mother, I went back home and became pretty much mute. I didn't want to talk. I became an introvert and held my feelings inside. My dad told me that I had to go back to school. I didn't want to go. My whole world had changed. How was I supposed to function in school? I woke up the next morning thinking it was all a bad dream. Nope it was reality. My dad drove my brother and me to school. I watched as my dad talked with my teacher. I hated the look on her face as she glanced over at me. I sat in my seat and waited. When I looked up my dad waved goodbye and my teacher was in my face. She gave me a sad frown face and shook her head like she understood. That school day was one of the hardest eight hour days I had to get through. I kept my mouth shut as my friends questioned me about where I had been and what had happened. They didn't need to know and they wouldn't understand.

After school my Aunt Dora picked me up and took me to her house. I tried to let go of the new found mute that had taken over my body when I saw my cousins but all I could do was cry. That night after a home cooked meal, my aunt sat with me and tried to lift my spirits. The words she spoke to me stung deep within and I struggled with them into adulthood. She said, "Baby, God won't put more on you than you can bear." "Really? God must really think I am strong," I thought. The whole night I could not get that phrase out of my head. I decided to talk to God myself and tell him I was not that strong. I could not bear what he had put on me. I wanted my mommy back. As I cried myself to sleep that night, I prayed that she would be all better in the morning.

At eight years old I thought losing my mom (as I knew her) to a stroke was the worst thing that could have ever happened to me. I did not realize that the strength and determination she showed each day would help me to see how strong I would become. My mom woke up each day with a big smile on her face. Even through the excruciating pain she felt, she smiled. She was in a single hospital bed alone. She would never sleep next to my father again. She would never walk again. Through her smile each day I saw her fight to live. She was there the best way she knew how. There were days when I would climb into her bed and take her "good" hand (her left side was paralyzed) and place it on my forehead. It was as if she took all of the pain and the worries of life away from me with just her touch. She endured so much pain while in that bed but she continued to show love to her family.

My brother became ill in 1987. He suffered from acute renal failure. My brother was my rock. He had been through everything with me. If there was ever a person that I could count on to know how I felt it was him. Although he was sick and had to go to dialysis three times a week, he still lived his life to the fullest. He went to school during the week and went out with friends on the weekends. I ran to him for comfort and solace when the man that I knew as my father, my rock, began a terrible journey down a road where many secrets were whispered and dark clouds began to circle. My father began using drugs. To me he was still my daddy. I didn't see him acting differently. I didn't feel him neglecting me or my family. I didn't believe it. The adults in my family were talking. I was older now so I heard what they said about my dad and I didn't like it one bit. He was the most generous, caring and strong man I knew. He was my superman. How could they assassinate his character like that? I didn't want to hear it and I didn't want to believe it, until one of those secrets became all too real for me. My father called me one day while I was staying with my aunt and uncle and he told me that his friend Sharon had had a baby girl. It was 1990, my senior year in high school. I don't know if I suppressed it, or I didn't hear it, but I didn't realize that this baby girl was my sister until several years later. My father was getting ready to move to another home and I was helping him pack. I found a bunch of letters and I was skimming through them to see if they should be kept or thrown away. There it was in black and white. I read his words, *I, Sidney began a relationship with Sharon and from that union a baby girl was born.* I felt like I had been electrocuted. I had watched this little girl. She was living with my aunt who had foster children. My dad would watch her from time to time, but she would go back to my aunt's house. He was still married to my mother who was living in a bed. I never confronted my father about his infidelity. My aunt told me that I had to understand that he was a man. He had done right by my mom but he was still a man and he had needs.

In 1994 my brother blessed our family with the birth of his only child, a baby girl named Ebone. She was the apple of his eye and mine too. Who would have known that his time with her would have been so short? It was November 18th 1996. I was at work at PG&E. My boss sat right behind me and she received a phone call. She answered and the caller hung up. Shortly after that the phone rang again. She answered and the caller asked to speak to me. She gave me the phone. It was my father. He said, "Brace yourself, your brother passed away." I screamed at the top of my lungs. I dropped the phone and ran to get my keys. I was out! My boss grabbed the phone and got the details of what had happened. My boss grabbed my hand and asked me to sit. She advised me she would take me to my dad's house. She talked to me the whole way to my dad's house. She was trying to calm me down. Initially, I thought the phone call was about my mom because she had been ill for so long. I think I was more prepared for that blow. I felt it was not my brother's time. He passed away from complications from his illness. He was only 26 years old. His death sent me into a tailspin. I didn't know who I was without him around. I was so depressed.

It was October 23, 1999. My little sister's ninth birthday. I had a party for her. We had a great day. She was happy and that was all that mattered. The truth of who this little girl was to me was shocking when I found out. I fell in love with her before I found out and although I was jealous of her.... I was my daddy's baby girl for 17 years! ...I wanted to make sure she was cared for. I could not let my sister grow up knowing that I resented her. So I fought hard to show her she was loved by me. After the party was over and she was playing with her new gifts, I climbed into my mother's bed and laid her right hand on my forehead like I had done so many times before. I did not know that that would be the last time I would ever get to do that. The next morning my phone rang early. I answered it. It was my dad on the other end. He said, "Your mother has died." I yelled at the top of my lungs, waking my roommate in the next room. She comforted me and took me to get food. She would not let me go to my parents' house until I was able to talk to her. I could not believe that a mere three years after my brother passed, my mother was gone. Depression set in once again but I learned to mask it. I continued on with life. I went to work. I finished school. I went out on the weekends. I lived life. Inside my heart was broken. I tried to be the example for my sister and my niece. I didn't want them to see me fall apart. I wanted to carry on the strength that my mother had shown me all of those years. Although all of those things were happening to my family I was determined to keep living. I began going to church. I realized that everything that had happened to me had actually happened for me. I was able to hear from GOD. I realized that through everything, HE was right there. HE carried me when I fell. HE continued to build my strength back up. Without HIM I would not be here. There were times I wanted to throw in the towel, but HE had given me the strength to endure. Although I have been through a lot, I continue to be patient and stand because I know that GOD isn't finished with me yet!

Sharice Porter Bio

Sharice Porter is the co-founder and co-owner of INPowerment University, where she helps young girls search within themselves to find the power that already lives within each of them. She obtained her Bachelor's Degree in Mass Communications from California State University, Hayward in 2002. While in school she wrote for the *Pioneer* - the campus newspaper and had aspirations of becoming a published author and speaker. As a young child she faced many hardships, the first of which changed the trajectory of her life...her mother had a stroke when Sharice was just eight years old. Sharice was always told to be seen and not heard and to stay out of grown folks business. What do you do when grown folks business becomes your business? You tend to grow up way before your time. With the struggles of her home life, she often struggled in school, but she was determined to make it to college. After college, she worked and helped to care for her family. In 2003, she accepted the Lord Jesus Christ as her Lord and savior and HE began to show her the reason behind all of the heartache and pain. She took a life changing solo trip to Hawaii in 2013 where she discovered her passion and began developing what would later become INPowerment University. With this platform she hopes to reach young girls that may feel hurt by what life has thrown at them. She wants them to realize the strength they need already lives inside of each of them.

Keilah Johnson

Age 37

East Bay Area, Ca

Mother-Author- Life Coach-Speaker-Teacher

Co-founder of "God's Perfect Hands-To FOCUS"

Co-Host/Panelist for "The Royal Court" Blog Talk Radio Show

Contact Information: MinisterKJohnson@gmail.com

"How I got over the Mess"

My name is Keilah Johnson. I am a 37-year-old single mother of three children and I will take you on my journey. I was raised in a two-parent home and I was preacher's kid. I have a child that is a product of rape. I have suffered from depression since I was a child. I have gone from having no electricity for a year growing up, to being homeless and moving from motel to motel; from living with friends to family members. I have been though many forms of abuse. I have had the person I was going to marry leave me, only to turn around and marry a close family member of mine less than a year later. That same family member plotted to drown me when we were younger.

You will go down memory lane of failed relationships, heartache and heart break. From let downs and disappointments to betrayal and addiction. My life, like any other, has not been squeaky clean, and I did not always make all the right decisions. But had it not been for all of those life and learning experiences, I would not have grown as much as I have into the woman I am today.

My main objective here is to reach someone who may have felt alone or maybe just silenced. Because of the life challenges I have experienced, I have chosen to break the silence and tell my story. I have always been told that someone needs to hear my story and that someone can benefit from hearing my story. I must admit, I was very withdrawn and apprehensive about sharing any part of my life story, but there are way too many silent people and not enough people speaking out and speaking up.

I never thought I would come out of my shell and talk about any of the things I have gone through or experienced. It took a lot for me to have the guts to share any of this. But one day I asked myself what benefit is it to stay in the dark? And what would I tell my younger self that would help her to become a better me? Had I known then what I know now, I probably could have avoided some major head on collisions in life.

My story may not be as unique as some, or as cookie cutter as others, but it is just that, my story. Every part of my life is a song. Music is what has helped me deal with the pain, hurt, sorry, sad times, low times, all the way to the pick-me-up moments, then on to the best and greatest and most memorable moments of my life. I want nothing less than the best for you. I want you to know that you are not alone in whatever situation you are in. Someone has gone through it and overcome it and is still here to tell the story of how they got over.

Growing up in the church did not make me any more protected from hurt, harm or danger. In fact, it made me more of a target. I felt I had to hide my feelings. I had to bury my emotions and I felt like I could never just be me around any and every one. I wasn't allowed to talk about everything. Learning to live in secret was not my preference, but it was the way it had to be. My parents did all they could and gave all they had. Still to this day they are right by my side. My younger brothers and I learned the importance of family and how to survive. We are all fighters. We are all survivors. Life doesn't always give you what you want, but you can bet you will get something you need out of life's experiences.

One of my first encounters with depression, deep depression was when I had first started my current job. I was very naive. I had pretty much lived a very sheltered life. I met this guy. He pretended to be interested in the things I was interested in. I was involved in an outside business and he always found ways to knock what I was doing or speak negatively. This should have been my first clue, but no. I ignored every red flag and warning sign. He then went from loving and caring and meeting my family, to being aggressive. What was happening?

I found myself having to fight. He physically attacked me. He was taking exactly what he wanted and did not care the cost.

He would no longer put on the facade of pretending to be a concerned, caring gentleman. I learned a lesson that day. All trust was broken. My spirit was now broken. I had become a shell of the former me. There was nothing anyone could say to bring me back. I had died spiritually.

From that point on I began to live in fear and was always on the defense. I shut down and did not know any other way to be. I wanted to just die. I wanted to be invisible and disappear in the background. To me, my life was over because of the hurt, the shame, and the embarrassment. How would I explain all of this? How would I face anyone or anything ever again? How could I let this happen? I was so stupid to put myself in that type of situation. I would never be the same person ever again. Then depression set in. I devalued myself. I depreciated my self-worth. I forgot that I was, and still am, a Queen. I had to tell myself that I would never ever be a victim ever again. I had to fight even harder for my sanity. I had to remind myself who I really was. It was a long, hard fight, but I never gave up.

Today, I am a teacher and leader who lets people know they can overcome their past. Reminding them of who they are and that their past does not define them and their future. In my upcoming book, "*How I Got Over. Finding and reclaiming the*

Queen in me," I will share the different ways to hold on and not lose sight of the winner in you.

Trust me, if I can overcome all of my junk and my past. So can you. Just knowing someone believes in you, without ever having met you should be motivation enough for you to wipe your eyes, get off your rusty dusty and start living your life again. Ask me how I know.

Keilah Johnson Bio:

Keilah Johnson is a Northern California resident, mother, singer, praise dancer, speaker, teacher and leader. She has worked in the court system for the last 16 years. She is one of the co-founders of "God's Perfect Hands-To FOCUS", a women's ministry focused on equipping women ages 18 and up to be kingdom minded women, walking in Christ as proper helpmeets, knowing who they are called to be in the body of Christ and teaching them to work together. She is currently the Executive Board Administrator of The Worship Crusade Chorale, and has held that position for the last 12 & 1/2 years.

Catch me on BlogTalk Radio:
www.Blogtalkradio.com/TheRoyalCourt
Co-Host/Panelist for "The Royal Court" Blog Talk Radio Show

Sharnice Marie Evans

Age 47

Author, Evangelist, Firebrand

Founder of Ladies on Purpose

"Standing in the Storm"

It was June 2015 when I started to notice the lack of intimacy. When I say intimacy, I'm referring to the basic show of affection from a man to a woman. A smile, a gentle touch, flirting, and cuddling. Soon after that it was the withholding of sex. When I questioned him, he would dismiss my concerns at first. Time would pass and I would question him again because there was no denying the obvious. He admitted that he was withholding himself from me due to him being upset. Actually he used the word mad. I asked, "Mad about what?" He said he had never truly gotten over an offense from two years ago. *"Really?"* I thought. You are harboring a two-year resentment? More recently he had been mad about me calling him an asshole. To be more specific, he was just unhappy in general with the direction of our marriage. His desire was to have a marriage that mirrored his parent's union. I interpreted his desire as him wanting me to be more submissive. I responded by saying that I submitted to the plan to close the doors of the church after two years of pastoring. I submitted to the idea of uprooting myself and children and leaving my job, friends and family to move to Stockton. I submitted to shutting down my personal ministry until further notice. I submitted to joining the church of his choice and sitting to receive more training that he thought we needed. How much more did I need to submit to prove my ability to submit? I expressed to him that his expectations were unreasonable and for him to withhold himself from me was ungodly and not biblical. He replied that this was the stand he was going to take until I would agree to his terms. Again, I thought, *"Really?!"* Knowing that this goes directly against what God says, you feel you have that right? He simply stated, without hesitation and quite coldly, that he would not argue the point with me and he did not intend to change his mind. At this point, I was at a complete loss for words. This was something I have never experienced. I thought to myself this is a new kind of devil.

I prayed and reached out to our marriage mentor for wise council. We both agreed that the seed of offense had been planted and been allowed to take root. He said the wise thing for me to do would be to apologize again for the offense and he gave me the exact Holy Ghost inspired words to say. He said if there would be any hope that the words that I spoke in meekness, humility, and sincerity would cause the wall that was built up to fall. Well, let me share with you the offense in question. About two years ago, my son found himself in trouble with the law and was placed on a court ordered curfew. He broke the curfew and my husband thought it was best to call the police and have my son returned to jail. Well, me being his mom, I was not having it. I felt that was an unnecessary measure to take. He had already spent 30 days in jail. My husband called the police and in defense of my son, I lied to the police and said what my husband was saying was untrue. I was acting as a mother protecting her son. My husband saw it as me undermining his authority. I was truly placed in a bad situation. In my sincere apology to my husband, I told him that I did love and respect him as the head of the house and that my decision was solely based on my need to protect my son. I asked that he forgive me for making him feel like I didn't respect him as the man of the house. He accepted my apology and said that we would talk further on the matter at a later date. I felt victorious in that area and saw that there was hope.

A week had passed and there had been no change in my husband's behavior. I thought, *"Wait a minute, you expressed your concern, I addressed your concern and there has been no change."* Well apparently it all goes back to the other issue of our marriage going into a different direction. He still insisted that he wanted our marriage to mirror his parents. I expressed to him that desire was antiquated. At the time I made that statement, he interpreted it as me calling his parents antiquated and as a direct insult. That was the nail in the coffin, along with me saying he was being an asshole. I called him an asshole because I had a dear friend who was homeless and needing a place to stay and my husband was placing so many rules and stipulations on her staying with us. I thought it was ridiculous, seeing that we were once in her position and we personally knew how it felt to be in that emotionally vulnerable state.

I began to do some research on "Sexless Marriages" and the root causes. I learned that it was a form of emotional abuse. We all know the importance of sex within the marriage. It is the highest form of intimacy and communication between a husband and wife. I was feeling more than just rejected. I was feeling abused in every sense of the word, and my research confirmed just that. It was an attempt of the enemy to do damage to my emotional well-being, self-esteem and self-worth. My husband was allowing the devil to trick him in this area. He bought into the lies that what he was doing was okay and that he was not in need of sex. At least not sex with me. It was more than just him being too mad to have sex, because I know men who will have sex right after an argument. He was operating in the spirit of offense, which is known to be one of the devil's devices that he uses to destroy relationships.

It became an emotional tug of war. I believe it was a power struggle. He said, "You do this, then I will give you that." I took the stand of what was right according to the Word of God, trying to appeal to his spiritual side. I told him that was not how God intended for marriage to be. I eventually said out of frustration that we might as well end it now because I can't give into your unrealistic demands. I was starting to feel bullied. I felt he would have gotten further with me by appealing to my emotions and by giving me what rightfully belonged to me - intimacy and sex.

In desperation I reached out to his family. First I reached out to an older sister, thinking that maybe since she was in a long-standing marriage, she could lend me some wise advice. After all, she had known him longer than I and she should be able to give me some insight. That turned out to be a huge mistake. Then I did what I felt was best and reached out to his sister who was also the assistant pastor at the church we attended. She told me that she never saw herself as our leader because we were showing signs of instability as church members. I took that as a direct insult. We pay our tithes, offering, and pledge, but because we missed a Sunday or two we were not seen as real members. I was appalled. However, she said she would talk to him to see where his head was. She called me back within minutes to inform me that he said he was tired. That he just wanted out of the marriage and would allow me time to move me and my son out. *"Really?! HE is tired?!"* I thought to myself. Five years of marriage and you're already tired. With you, I have endured homelessness and financial instability, and *YOU* are tired? It was almost laughable. She said it so calmly it was almost scary. She didn't even ask to pray with me or bother to say that she would be praying for me. I thought the whole thing was quite odd.

All of this took place on a Saturday night. Nothing was even discussed between my husband and I. We just went to bed and got up the following morning and went to church as usual. In the meantime, I had a speaking engagement in Mississippi that was in limbo because I didn't know the status of my marriage. Well now that I had clarity I saw that as a green light to keep my word and go.

That Sunday in church was very uncomfortable. How can I worship beside the man who was choosing to leave me? I couldn't. I sent him a text right there during service telling him that this will be the last Sunday for me at that church. After all, how could I sit under leaders who didn't see the need to be

98

more assertive when it came to the demise of my marriage? I left that night to prepare for my departure for Mississippi. When it dawned on him what my plans were, the text messages started. I was on the Greyhound bus receiving messages that he was planning to put my son and I out while I was in Mississippi. This is one of the actual text conversations:

***Him talking*:** By the time you get back to Stockton I will need to know if you are planning on staying here or moving back to Antioch. If your plans are to remain in the house then I will be relocating elsewhere but, if you are moving then I will keep the place. We will no longer co-habit together; I think it's best we go our separate ways. If you are staying I will be removing my things. I don't know what made you feel like the people you called would change my mind and, calling Pastor Dew was not the business...

***My response*:** It's so sad that you would rather walk in defeat then to believe in the infallible God that you serve for restoration. I will not be moving.

***Him talking*:** After all the people that you call and talk to about me saying that I had a problem you going to stand here and tell me that I'm walking in defeat I think you should reevaluate what has been going on I'm not always wrong and I'm not wrong in this you betrayed me you don't went behind my back you want against what I said and what I believe and I'm still walking in defeat you should study to show yourself approved to God. Rents due on the first you got get pge turned on in your name and whatever cable system you planning on having

My response: Yes defeat. And what you are doing far trumps whatever you think I've done. You are abandoning the marriage, breaking covenant with me and God. You have NO BIBLICAL grounds for what you are doing. And with God we will manage just fine. I never told anyone you had a problem other than the problem you had with me. You haven't been willing to sit and discuss and reason with me. You're tired. Your actions are spiteful and cruel. But that's between you and God. Just for the record I love you and am not in agreement with ending the marriage.

Him talking: So I guess Pastor Charles I guess my sister sherry and I guess my friend Pastor Dew was lying when they told me that you call them and talk to them about me and my issues that's all I have to say have a good day

My response: You call it talking about your issues and I call it reaching out for help. And nothing I said was slanderous or untrue. I never talk to Pastor Charles other than the other day when you were threatening to put me and Shaddai out. You have a good day.

End of Conversation

Now mind you I was on assignment, wanting to keep my word and fulfill my obligation. I reached out to the leaders of the church with no avail. So I had to reach out and involve family. They managed to calm him down to the point that he agreed not to remove me and my son from the home because I told them to tell him I was prepared to involve the police.

When I finally returned home, I came home to a lock on my bedroom door. He had moved me into my son's room and the environment was hostile. There was very little to talk about and much to pray about. My stand was that I loved my husband, I wanted my marriage and I was willing and ready to fight for it. I reached out to a couple that had counseled us in the past and explained to them what was going on. The husband called my husband and I could hear the conversation in the other room. I could hear my husband making reference to knowing what God could do, but he wasn't willing to put any more work into making things better. I also heard him agree to us meeting with them. I felt hopeful. I talked to the wife and she told me to pray and ask God what was my part in this whole demise. I agreed that I would, although I couldn't honestly see that I had done anything that could have possibly brought us to this place. I had asked my husband when he set up our appointment for. He said "we don't have an appointment. You must think I'm playing, I'm leaving you!"

I had prayed the prayer, and like always God responded. God showed me two things specifically that I had done. I repented to God, and then I immediately called my husband and apologized to him and asked his forgiveness. He accepted the apology and said that he forgave me. Still there was no visible change.

I went to a local church from an invite by someone who had been through a similar situation. In my time of worship and crying out to the Lord, a Prophetess laid hands on me and spoke these reassuring words directly into my spirit. She said, "God will restore, it will be better than before. You will have to stand quietly; do not put my hands on it." All I could do was sob as I literally laid my head in God's lap. I then went to a women's retreat and another prophetess laid hands on me and spoke these words into my spirit. She said, "God is dealing with my husband right now in the area of wisdom, and God is going to my house and cleaning things up". Once again I sobbed in the lap of God.

Since then, I was led back to a church where I knew that I would hear directly from God and the man and woman of God had the ability to talk directly to my spirit. The Refiners House. My first Sunday back God used the man of God to speak directly to my emotion and desire to remain in my marriage and fight for my husband's return, not only to the marriage but to his place in God. He went on to confirm that God was turning things around and this trial was only strengthening me as a Prophetess to the nations. The anointing on my life was only being made richer and I was only going higher in the things of God because of the attack. I got up off the floor just that much stronger and even more prepared to fight.

I have been quiet during my time of devastation. I have not allowed my emotions to dictate my actions. I have approached every conflict in a Godly manner. I am allowing God to work some things out in me during this very painful time in my life. Currently it would appear that my husband is comfortable in his transgression and he is attending a church that does not challenge his choices. I had to forgive him, as well as, those who would appear to be upholding his decision. When I say uphold is decision, I mean that they are not insisting that he would fight to stay in the marriage. People have taken a passive stand.

We are currently living together in the same house as roommates, which has been very difficult for me emotionally. He has shown me no signs of wanting to reconcile, but I have learned to not see things as they are, but as what God has promised me that they will be. I am learning to trust God on a whole other level. I am determined to do things differently this time. I am doing things God's way in order to receive God's results. I'm choosing not to use any manipulation and I am keeping my motives pure in regards to my husband and our marriage. I don't want temporary results but I'm looking to reap lifetime benefits in my marriage. This attack was designed, and allowed, by God to Reposition us for our Purpose and to put us back in the right relationship with our Promise. I know that God is going to do IT IMMEDIATELY (Mathew 14:31)!

In the mean time I remain in the position of prayer. I have been blessed to be able to continue to parent my two youngest sons, hold a full time job, return to school to receive my B.A degree in Business Leadership, start my t-shirt line and now I have been given the opportunity to tell my story. I don't know when or how this will conclude, but I do know that it will conclude with me being victorious and reconciled back with my husband. You need to be encouraged in knowing that what has come to break you will only succeed in making you.

Lady Sharnice Marie Evans Bio
Exhorter and Servant of God
Founder of Ladies on Purpose

Sharnice is a Prophet to the Nations, Prayer Warrior, Exhorter, Teacher and Preacher. Most importantly she loves God and His people. Her mission in life is to empower people to discover and walk in their purpose. She is a mother of four, a grandmother of two and has been married for almost six years. The pain that she has endured and overcome in life has birthed her out into true ministry. She recently pastured, alongside her husband, in the city of Antioch for two years. While pasturing, she had the opportunity to affect change in the lives of many, as well as, a dying community. She is the founder of Ladies on Purpose, which is a Ministry that was birthed to assist men and women in discovering their purpose through God's Word and the power of Deliverance. She is a survivor of domestic violence, abandonment, and homelessness and truly knows what it means to never give up. She has allowed life's challenges to make her and not break her. Sharnice is passionate about helping people and she incites change by taking radical actions to bring about that change. Sharnice is currently pursuing her B.A Degree in Business Leadership while at the same time launching her t-shirt line "Kingdom Dwellers". God has ordained and purposed her to uniquely minister to the hearts of hurting women, not only locally, but internationally. She has been through the war but is not torn and has allowed her pain to push her to her purpose. It is her humble desire to be used by God in total submission.

Denese Dillihant

Age 23

Motivational Speaker-Singer-Author-Entrepreneur

Pittsburg,Ca

Follow me on FB @Denese Dillihant

Email: Denesecolquitt@gmail.com for Bookings & Events

"The Prodigal Daughter"

"Come on Denese, you know what this is." He said to me confidently. As I sat there and stared back at him, I tried to hide the unwavering truth… I had no idea what I was looking at. He had confidence in the façade I had put up, so I wasn't going to ruin it by simply asking him what it was. With a devious smirk plastered on my face, I began to list all the possible things it could be. So the obvious was that it was a drug, but which one I could not tell so I stared long and hard as he took the broken glass pipe, no longer than my pinky finger, and lit the pebble sized white rock that he placed on it. I watched the way the flame consumed it and how he inhaled the smoke that traveled visibly through the pipe. I watched the way his body instantly became relaxed. It was actually quite mesmerizing. Although a slight feeling of fear tried to enter my mind, excitement, and the now overwhelming feeling to get high, trampled the fear drastically. As he handed me the pipe with this now burnt substance, I neither hesitated nor questioned anything. I smiled with gratitude and happily lit, inhaled, and exhaled. That night, in the passenger seat of a small white Honda, I smoked crack cocaine for the first time. I was seventeen years old, and unfortunately for me, it wouldn't be the last time. (Ok so let's pause for a second here. If you are anywhere near in your right mind reading this, you are probably thinking, "What has to go wrong in one's life for them to be smoking crack at 17??" I know. I know. Let's go back a few years, where it may have all started.)

Growing up, I was never what you would call a troubled child. I had what one would call a troubled childhood. I was the middle child of three girls from my mother and my father. The oldest girl is my twin. My parents kept us in church from babies on up. My grandparents started their church when I was seven, so church was a big part of my childhood. My parents did their absolute best with us, but their best together was mediocre at best, in my opinion. My parents fought constantly and I watched my mother be abused their whole relationship. My father was a heavy alcoholic and had an extremely hard time keeping his hands to himself. He was also a big time cheater. But with all his flaws and imperfections, my father was my very own superhero and I was his baby. We did everything together, including drinking at a very young age. My parents divorced when I was eleven. And the thought of not being with my father tore my heart to pieces. I was forced to live with my mother, whom I had now grown to resent.

From the age of eleven through fifteen I went through major physical, mental and spiritual changes. My mother was a great provider during this time, but emotionally she was distant and very unstable. By this time she had gotten remarried to a preacher. He was all right, but he was not my father. I made various attempts to live with my father, but they all failed. So I started running away from home at fifteen. I also started smoking weed and drinking excessively. I would go to class high and drunk, just about every day. I skipped half of my classes to get high. From tenth grade to my senior year, I barely maintained a 1.9 GPA. This was drastically different from the straight A student I was in elementary and middle school.

I became someone completely different and I liked it. I became rebellious and cold. I also began having sex at fifteen with what I now call my first love. This opened a door within myself that should have never been opened. I was not ready to handle such mature activities at such a young age. I became a "loose" girl. I would drink to get so drunk that I would have sex with anyone as long as they kept me "out of my mind." This lifestyle led me right into the arms of the man who gave me crack cocaine for the first time. At seventeen, I had a huge fight with my mother and left for good. I ran away to my new guy. A man I had only known through conversations over the phone for a couple weeks. I moved in with him the night I left my mother's house. I now had the freedom and the love I felt I was desperately missing. I was so empty inside and needed someone to love and someone to love me. This man gave me everything I wanted. He spoiled me like no one had ever done before. And he gave me whatever drugs I wanted whenever I wanted. But getting everything I wanted from him came at a heavy price.

After a month of the "good life" everything suddenly changed. He began beating me. Not just a slap or a little shove. He began choking me until I passed out, biting me until I screamed, pulling my hair and dragging me and abusing me any way he could. These moments came in between highs. As though I were the blame for everything going wrong in his life, he beat me, relentlessly. After the abuse started, we got kicked out of where we were staying and became homeless. Amazingly though, I was still madly in love with him and leaving him never crossed my mind. We were a regular Bonnie and Clyde. I told him I would follow him to the end of the earth, and at the time I really meant it. We stole together, got high together, and ran and slept on the streets together. We were inseparable and I was all the way out my mind. Until one day, I woke up. At eighteen years old, I was sleeping in a church my boyfriend and I had broken into. The weight of the world hit me so hard that night. Harder than any punch my man had ever thrown me. And that night I broke and cried like never before. I crawled to the altar and screamed, "I want my mommy! I want my life back! God, if there is a God, I need you now!!" God spoke to me for the first time that night and I instantly became joyful. I felt Him all over me and I couldn't stop laughing. It was an insane feeling that felt better than any high. This feeling was accompanied with blessed assurance and divine clarity.

The next day, I ran away from my boyfriend, got on a train and went home to my mother. I had a warrant for my arrest, so my mom gave me a few days then took me to jail. I turned myself in and stayed in the county jail for two and a half months. I found out I was pregnant in jail. This was now the beginning of 2011. After jail time I was released on probation. And just a couple months later, I violated. Now six months pregnant, I was sent to juvenile hall for this charge. I stayed there for a month and got released to an intensive in-home rehabilitation. I was now seven months pregnant. I was sentenced to stay there for eighteen months, but I ended up getting kicked out of there after two months. By the grace of God, I went to court and I got sent to my grandmother's house and sentenced to finish my time in an outpatient rehab. During this time I went to church a lot and gave my life completely over to God. My grandmother prayed for me, day in and day out. Then October 5th 2011, my first son was born. A couple of months later we got our own home with the help of my grandparents. I was back to school and working in the ministry; my life was turning around.

During this time I made up in my mind I would never go back to the life I was living. I would never go back to the man who beat me. I would do all that I could to give my son the life he deserved. I made the decision and I followed through. I dated a bit in between and stayed off the hard drugs for good and then in January 2013, I met the love of my life. A little preacher from Richmond, California. He seemed to have dropped out of nowhere right into my life. He was handsome, funny, and one of the realist people I had ever met. He pursued me like no one had ever done before. He went to my family and asked for my hand in marriage. He proposed to me just a couple months later, in April 2013, and we married May 5, 2013. I didn't have to compromise anything to be with him; he made me better in every area of my life. That's how I knew he was the one. He moved me and my son into his home, gave me his car, and loved me like no one had ever loved me before. We prayed together, read scripture together, and our lives became nothing but love and ministry. He took my son in as his own. My son's biological father chose not to be in my son's life, but God had another plan for his life. Then in January 2014, we started our own church called "Powerhouse Holiness Church." I also started a women's organization called, "First Lady Standards," during this time.

At this point in my life, God had completely delivered me from all of my troubles. He snatched me out of the darkness and literally made me to be a light to this dark world. It was during this time that I realized I could not take my sobriety for granted, even with all that I was now doing and how far I had come. I realized I had to wake up every morning and choose sobriety, choose life, and choose freedom. I attended Bible College during this time, as well. Then the next year, God blessed us with another son, Henry Louis Dillihant IV, born February 16, 2015. Everything in my life had completely changed. I became an entrepreneur and stopped attending college for a while and worked from home raising my little kings. And now a year after our second son, God has blessed us with another child, our princess, Halo London'Dior Dillihant.

So to sum up my life now, just six years after that first hit, I am 23 years old, married with three beautiful children. I would have never thought I would be such a great mommy or that I'd have so many so young (LOL!). But I've found out that one of my greatest callings in life is motherhood. It's a lifetime assignment and I thank God for allowing me to experience it in this lifetime. And my husband is so amazing. He makes marriage and motherhood both challenging and fun. I am also a motivational speaker, writer, gospel recording artist, minister of music, entrepreneur and true follower of Jesus Christ. My mother and I are best friends now! God restored and rebuilt our relationship. We pray together and I go to her for EVERYTHING. God will restore relationships with loved ones you forfeited for a life that was no good, no matter what you did or how far you went. My mother and stepfather have their own church as well, and they are devoted to seeing people's lives changed for the better.

Looking back, I believe I should have lost my mind in those streets, but God kept me for such a time as this. God loved me when I didn't love myself. God preserved my mind, through His word. I began reading the scriptures for myself during my jail and rehab time and have continued to this day. And the only thing still keeping me together today is God. Left to my own devices I would break down and die. I gave up everything to follow Him, and He has never failed me. I gave up sleeping around, drinking, smoking and partying at a young age because

I found out God had a better life for me and all I needed to do was walk in it.

I made the decision to live right the best I know how and I haven't looked back yet. I lost the friends I had when I made that decision. I got talked about a lot, still do, because I made that decision. I get misunderstood a lot, because of that decision. But none of that matters to me, my freedom in Jesus Christ means more to me than this old world. I was addicted, bound to bad habits and bad people . . . and on today . . . I AM FREE. I pray if you are struggling with any type of addiction that the Lord free you and give you the power to overcome it! He is able, He did it for me and I know He can do it for you! Give Him your all today and watch your life become a miracle.

Denese Dillihant Bio:

Denese Dillihant was born in Northern California, in the city of Walnut Creek. She was raised in the city of Pittsburg, Ca. She grew up in a home where domestic violence was prevalent. Denese found positive ways at an early age to channel her emotions. She began singing as soon as she could talk and loved music from infancy. As she grew older she began singing in the church choir and leading songs and singing solos. She started writing songs as well. Denese began playing the alto sax at eleven years old and continued to play well into high school where she was a faithful member of the Pittsburg High School marching show band. Denese was a very active and athletic child and won many awards and certificates playing basketball. She graduated from Pittsburg High School in 2010. All of her activities and accomplishments didn't stop her from feeling abandoned and empty throughout her teens. After high school, her life took many turns in different avenues that would lead her down many paths, some dangerous and almost cost her her life. She became a teenage single mother and battled drugs and alcohol addiction. Denese made a decision to change her life forever one day to be a better person for her baby son. She chose to be free. She attended and completed a year, and received a certificate of sobriety, in January of 2012 from Ujima Outpatient Recovery Center in Pittsburg,Ca. She then started Bible College at Patton University in Oakland, California. Her specific area of study was Biblical Education/Studies. She would later transfer schools to the Bay Area School of Urban Missions, where she is currently pursuing her degree in Biblical Studies and Evangelism. She has the heart of an outreach person working to help others recover from whatever life has them bound in. Denese is now married with three small children and runs a home-based business. She started a young women's organization called, "First Lady Standards," in 2014, and has weekly classes for women of all ages. Her mission is to create tomorrow's prestigious women by transforming the lives and minds of today's young women. Her purpose is to elevate the standards in the minds of young women by developing and enhancing self-worth, providing spiritual guidance, and establishing a safe haven for positive change. Her goal is to demolish child/adult prostitution, domestic violence, drug addiction, physical and mental abuse, financial instability, dysfunctional relationships, and bad health among today's young women. She hosts many community events and loves feeding and clothing the needy. Denese loves to love on people and in everything she does she seeks to please God. At 23 years old she is confident she is on the path God has laid out for her. She has plans of opening a home for teenage mothers in recovery to further fulfill her calling in life. And she is releasing her very own worship CD and book, *Somebody's Baby*, in Fall 2016. She is a featured author in the empowering book compilation, *Breaking Through Barriers*, releasing in July 2016.

"I'm living to inspire a generation, and change a nation."

- Denese Dillihant

Rachel "Motivates You" Edwards

Age 44

Entrepreneur, Life and Motivational Consultant

Business Email: womenofvirtueorganization@gmail.com

Business Mobile Phone: (916) 399-3413

Sacramento, Ca

"A Woman of Virtue Found"

"When you open your heart to God and let your yes mean yes, you will turn your mess into a message."

-Rachel Edwards

<u>My Mess</u>

It was a chilly day in January and I just finished getting dressed. I was wearing a black suit with pink pinned-strips with black heels. I styled my hair in its natural curls because it was the quickest way to style my hair when I was pressed for time like today. Sometimes I wonder if I'm the only one who sets five different alarms five minutes apart...smh. To say the least, this day was very special, in fact, one of the most unforgettable events was about to take place in my life today. I was about to meet with my first client at the mental health center. Yes, *"my* client." And I have to admit I was a little nervous because although I had completed all courses for the Master's in Counseling/Marriage & Family Therapist program with high scores and a 3.56 GPA, I was still apprehensive about meeting with an actual client. I had a deep feeling the meeting would be much different then the role-playing my cohort and I conducted in class.

Yet, I was still excited and eager to meet my client no matter how many butterflies formed in my stomach. That was one thing I would soon realize about myself, I had an inner strength that could not be destroyed by any circumstance I faced. I guess this is why I didn't think twice about running out to the nearby Walgreen's to buy a bottle of Maybelline's 340 *Fit Me Foundation* and some concealer. "Never forget the concealer," I whispered. The combination works a miracle, especially to hide a black eye. "Maybe if I would've kept my mouth closed, things wouldn't have gotten so bad. Lord! Now I have to go to this store and I have to go before I'm late." I wasn't a makeup person, but I did keep a bottle of foundation and concealer for episodes like this one.

It was Sunday, and as usual my husband, an avid alcoholic, came home "feelin' himself". If you don't know what that means, it's slang for having a big head at any given moment.

My breathing got a little short and butterflies formed in the pit of my stomach as I thought about the incident that occurred three nights prior. The Bay Area made the night chilly. He (my husband) was gone as usual, making sure to leave before I get home from work (though sometimes he would wait until I got home only to leave 30 minutes later). When arguing, he would say at least he waited for me to come home, although he would be gone until the next morning. I lose count of how many nights I spent in a lonely bed, wondering where the man I married was, who he was with, what (or who, keeping it real) he was doing. But of all the cheating, alcohol was his biggest infidelity.

I still reminisce today about looking at the clock right before leaving work wondering if this was going to be one of those disastrous days. Would it be cool and calm or devastating? I sometimes dreaded going home. Sometimes, even when things went well, I had already prepped myself for a fight. However, on this particular evening, being the weekend before my big day, he was already drinking early that morning. I could tell because by 10 am that morning he called and said he needed to make a run. That usually meant him going around the corner to one of his drinking buddies' houses. No food, just his morning 211 Steel Reserve malt liquor, which is widely known to make it consumers act crazy. Then following the 211, he would get a fifth of peach Amsterdam, maybe even two-fifths.

Yes, my husband was an alcoholic and I was very familiar with his regimen. In addition, he was the type who would attend many AA meetings and programs, yet would get absolutely nothing out of it. He would justify his non-acceptance by saying it was just a waste of time or he would find something wrong with the facilitators. I can't say how many times we discussed why he wouldn't work on his drinking. It simply got to the point where if I said anything about his drinking, he would defensively say I needed to work on my anger.

Anyway, it was Friday night and I was happy it was the weekend. I would spend a little time on Saturday preparing to meet my first client on Monday afternoon. I gathered my helpful hints that my practicum professor gave to us, along with other resources I collected throughout the Master's program from other teachers, online and cohort classmates. I was prepared. A smile came on my face as I put on the black suit with pink pin strips. I pulled my black flats from the closet and sat them in front of the dresser. I wanted everything ready for Monday. A smile appeared on my face as I took one last peek at the whole outfit, "Yes!" was what I said in a medium tone. Suddenly it was as though someone took an eraser and wiped my smile right off my face. My heart started pounding, the butterflies in my stomach were fluttering at high speed and my palms were sweaty as I heard the vicious slamming at the front door. My two youngest children, who were seven and nine at the time, ran in my room with panic. Their eyes bugged open as they whispered, "I think it's my dad." I instructed my second oldest child to go open the door before he broke it down. Although she was hesitant, she did as she was told.

I mentally prepared myself. As usual he headed right into the kitchen to put his drink in the refrigerator before heading into the garage. In the next five minutes, loud music came into the room. The sounds of hardcore rap, with all that profanity and torture for me. I didn't want my kids hearing that stuff. I didn't want to hear it either.

I don't really remember everything. I know he called for me to come in the garage. He was either calling for me or one of the kids. I was just so irritated, hurt, fed up, disappointed... however you name it I was it. I just wanted to have a husband who put his family first. I loved my husband and believed God would change him if I would just keep the faith. So as I entered the garage, he began to say that he didn't want to be together anymore and that he knew I could do better. My blood boiled with anger. I could feel it rising though I tried to contain my fury. He continued to talk meaningless things and just ramble on about how work and school took away from the family. How he was there with the kids every day. By this time, I had enough and I begin to defend my stance about being the bread winner of this family. I reminded him that I started school when he was in prison and that earning my degree was what

God had called me to do. But it was like talking to a brick wall. He stumbled around the garage in his drunkenness, stumbled over the bag of cans not even bothering to pick them up as they rolled everywhere. I couldn't take it anymore, so I began to walk away. As I did, he began to call me all types of derogatory names. I ignored him and went back upstairs and closed my room door. Just a few minutes later he busted in the room and stormed in the closet to get a jacket. I didn't say anything. He was mumbling cuss words about me. I could feel my ears getting hot, my heartbeat racing, and my palms sweating. There was a sense of fear that came over me, warning that something was about to happen. My papers from school that were sitting on my desk flew passed me landing on the bed and floor as he swung his arm knocking over everything in sight. I got up and asked him to just leave. I remember his piercing eyes looking at me as I stood facing him. His 6 foot 4 slender body stood hovering over my 5'2 frame. Stars flashed before my eyes, and the room spun. I stumbled backwards just as the bed stopped me from falling to the floor. The side of my face was throbbing and I could feel a knot just below my right eye. I couldn't open it (my eye). I held it as I walked to the mirror. "Oh no!" I thought.

He walked out of the room. As usual, once he did something harsh, he went back into the garage until things cooled down. I made my way downstairs. Being extra careful not to let the kids see what happened. I hurried to the kitchen to get ice or a bag of frozen veggies and a towel from the linen closet. As I tiptoed back upstairs, I could hear my kids whispering. Tears formed in my eyes as I hurried back into my room and closed the door. My thoughts were all over the place. How would I get this eye down by Monday? Even my efforts to hide it from the kids didn't work. They knew the routine better than I did. One by one each of them eased into my room asking if I was ok. All I would think is "How could God keep allowing this happen to us and why was He taking so long to answer my prayers and save my husband?" Little did I know it would be only a little over a year before God would deliver me from this bondage.

My Message

I was sitting with my client. She was a 44 year old mother of five children. As she begin to pour out her troubles and share about the childhood abuse, the thoughts of my own troubles went into remission. I was a counselor. But it wasn't her tales of her being molested that touched me; it was her sharing stories about the mental, physical, and emotional abuse by her husband. She cried as she explained how he manipulated family members (and mutual friends) into believing their problems were her fault, how he would complain she pressured him which led to him wanting to leave home (even his infidelity). This woman, not too much older than me poured her heart out as tears flowed. I can't explain what I saw, but there rose a lump in my throat and a knot in my stomach as I continued to listen. I excused myself to get tissue for her and to create time to regroup. "This woman needed guidance, not someone to encourage pity." I told myself as I walked back into the room. When I heard the words, "I want to give up." depart from her lips, something happened on the inside of me. It was almost like reflex. I begin to talk to her, expressing feelings of empathy. Before long she was laughing again saying she hadn't laughed in a long time; that she was so glad she came to counseling. After confirming our next appointment she left and I completed notes. Although my first counseling session was over, my outlook of my personal life was different. There was something on the inside of me that felt like a fireball that needed to be released. Something was going to happen, but I didn't know what.

It was January 2015 and I was on the 21 Day Daniel Fast. As usual, all hell was breaking loose. Though my husband and I were not arguing as much, you could feel the tension in the atmosphere. I was tired, stressed out, angry. Not because I was still waiting for my husband to be delivered, but because I was still in this circumstance. I now desired out of my turmoil. "Lord, Help Me Please!" This was my plea, not saving prayers for my husband. Yet, I was confused about how my attitude switched so quickly. What happened? I don't know but I was starving for more of this new feeling. I had prayed, fasted, cried, pleaded and begged God to save him, but God didn't. The marriage became a stronghold. I begin to believe I was in bondage for years; that my husband was my biggest and most dangerous stumbling block.

It was late evening and I was sitting in the living room. My husband had left as usual, already drunk and had called one of his drinking buddies to pick him up. It was no surprise that he would start an argument just to get out the house, or better yet, to distract from his ulterior motive. You would've thought he'd learn that this scheme of his no longer worked, yet he continued to start havoc nevertheless. Whether it was with one of the children or myself, it didn't matter much to him. It was as though there was a gratification for having the house in an uproar. But something was different. I was numb it seemed. It stopped bothering me about him being gone. I no longer cared when he left. In fact, that was an opportunity for peace in the house and quiet time for me with the kids and God. I didn't understand this new feeling I had. What was it?

For a while after the last altercation, which could have left me damaged for life, I wondered why the Lord allowed all of this hurt and pain in my life. I supported my husband, I worked hard to provide for us, I paid all the bills. I became very angry with God for allowing the pain in my life. I didn't understand how a God would allow me to go through this when His word promised to protect and keep me if I'd receive Him into my heart. So I demanded to know why. Why? One morning I woke up, it was about 5:30 am. I called into a prayer line facilitated by Dr. Lakita Long. This would be God's beginning of a great process in me. As I begin to read scriptures and talk to God more, I became stronger in dealing with what happened to me. But I still had questions about why my marriage was so poisoned and why I had to suffer pain and disgrace. One day I was talking to a young woman who was friends with my sister. She spoke to me about her current situation. And as she did I could see so many similarities with my own circumstances. I won't go into details about her situation. I will leave it for her to tell her own story (which one day I believe she will). But as I began to talk to her more and more, I realized it was because of my sharing of my story and my ability to personally relate and sympathize with all the emotions she was feeling, she was able to get out of her abusive relationship and move on. Witnessing this great transition in this young woman's life allowed me to see just why God allowed me to go through what I went through. If I had not gone through it, I wouldn't be able to relate to what women in these circumstances go through and I would probably not have the drive and passion to help them. How could I be mad at God for giving me this opportunity to feel these women's pain and suffering up close and personal, while assisting them, possibly saving their life?

I am now the Founder and Director of *Women of Virtue Org*, an organization for the wellness of women, children and communities. *Women of Virtue*'s mission is to help women and children achieve success in full circle (the whole person), mentally, physically, emotionally and spiritually. *Women of Virtue* is designed to assist in the recognition of abilities and encourage them to reach their full potential. I'm now driven to help children develop heath - mentally and emotionally; to help women overcome stumbling blocks that have hindered them for too long so that they may know their true value and worth. There are many programs within *Women of Virtue*, including a writing group, called *Women of Virtue Writing Group*. Since beginning the writing group in October 2015, we now have 40 women from many different walks of life. All who have actually come out and shared, have powerful stories of triumphs. As I share my story with each of them, including how I was led to start *Women of Virtue* and the writing group, many of them give feedback about how grateful they are for the group and how they want to assist in the whole organization. Many of the women have verbally expressed recognition of what they view as a power and strength within me, especially after sharing the final altercation between my husband and I. I am extremely grateful that God has placed many creative, intelligent and strong women in my life with the same passion and drive that I have. I am honored to have been in the same circle as some of these Women of God.

My message for the woman is that we all have marketable abilities to be shared and used as a service for others. All we have to do is say "Yes" to God and open our heart to Him.

Today, I have standards that I refuse to compromise just for anyone, especially a man. I am currently working on a book that I refer to as a "tool" for women who have fallen victim to thinking they need to be validated by a man. I share parts of my story as I help women to recognize abuse and how to walk away from it (including coping with the aftermath) and gain/regain control over their lives. The book is due to be released in 2017. I'm here to let my sisters know that nobody can validate them. In fact, you were beautifully and wonderfully made in God's image. There's nobody else like you in this world, so you see, there's no need for validation. One of the ladies in my writing group said "Pain is inevitable but suffering is optional."

Rachel "Motivates You" Edwards Bio:
Entrepreneur, Life and Motivational Consultant, Motivator

Rachel M Edwards is a native of the Bay Area, born and raised in Pittsburg, California. She is the youngest of seven children and the mother of four; Ragene, 20; DaJanae, 16; Dandre, 11 and Mikaylah, 9. Rachel is recently divorced after 14 years of marriage.

Rachel has worked in the administrative field for over 20 years and in the counseling field for about ten years, which includes mental health, addictive and Christian counseling.

Rachel's desire for outreach was inspired when she co-organized conferences with Pastor Mechelle Rabot, Founder of *DIVAS By Design International*, an organization for women suffering with issues from addiction and abuse to suicide. Rachel worked with Pastor Mechelle for 15+ years, and as an assistant and co-organizer of the conferences for three years.

Rachel holds a Bachelor's of Science in Business Management and a Master's in Counseling. She is currently a registered Marriage and Family Therapist Intern in the state of California. One of her future goals is to become a licensed Marriage and Family Therapist (MFT) in California.

Rachel is also the Founder and Director of *Women of Virtue Organization,* an organization designed to improve the health and wellness of women, children and their families. She believes the organization to be a divinely appointed assignment to serve the community by helping those in need to reach their full potential. She refers to the Power for 4-E's, Educate, Equip, Empower and Encourage as the key to help accomplish the mission of *Women of Virtue* and refers to herself as the "The Motivator".

Rachel has experienced many trials and hardship. She is a domestic violence survivor, has overcome depression, low self-esteem and anxiety. However, she explains that through her experience, both professional and personal, she is determined to help women who are currently facing or who are recovering from similar circumstances. She will be launching her life consulting business, Empowered Living Life Consulting in 2016.

The Take Away (Epilogue)

To end this amazing book, I thought it would be awesome to point out some words of wisdom, or messages, featured in each story. There is definitely more than one message in each story. This book features amazing women from different walks of walk with their ages ranging from 23-47. In my experiences, I believe wisdom is a purely internal thing as we learn lessons at all ages, but the wisdom we gain from learned lessons is the beauty added to the message.

Tanicia "Shamay Speaks" Currie:

"Accountability then forgiveness then healing is where true growth occurs"

"We cannot blame others for personal choices we made especially with our bodies and relationships. Ask yourself, how can one truly heal if they do not acknowledge any accountability for their own choices?"

"I had to forgive myself within first. You have to deal with the reality that you control your thoughts and your choices, not other people. If we allow others to control our thoughts and harbor grudges, we stop our internal growth."

"There was beauty in my dark moment and there can be in yours. Whatever situation you're facing or dealing with, be sure to own your truth in it, learn to cope, and move forward. Once you can learn with every bad situation to be accountable, forgive, and heal, your life will continue to shift to a better place."

Megan Anderson:

"I may be wounded and have scar upon scar. I will continue to make mistakes. But those mistakes don't make me. What makes me now, is how I choose to rebuild."

"I am still on the path to discovering what a broken woman loves. Yes, I say that I am 'broken'. Being broken does not mean that I will be broken forever or that I cannot be mended. I am beautifully broken and I now look at the positive choices I make as the glue that puts the pieces of me back together."

Danae Braggs:

"I prayed this elaborately specific prayer about what I wanted/needed my husband to be and I failed to mention his name. The darkness had been lightened. My mind was no longer clouded by the transference of negative energy, secrets and the "what ifs" of failure. Once I let go God blessed me with everything that I asked for and then some."

"In order to sharpen a skill or perfect a craft one needs clarity. At this point clarity was what I was missing for the past 14 plus years. In the midst of my life falling apart God gave me clarity."

Philicia Jones:

"I want people to understand that whatever you go through in life be strong through the situation and if you can make it through, you're a victor and not still a victim."

"Don't let anyone, not even your superiors, tell you not to report any abuse. Even if it's verbal it all hurts the same in the end. Love yourself first and foremost because no one can love you like you can."

Keisha Frowner:

"This is not what I wanted, but had to do what was best for my children. Yes I am a living witness. I refused to be a victim no matter how long it took to get on my feet. You too can persevere and not let your circumstances hold you back. Leaving was not easy, and yes I was afraid, but God gave me the courage to do it. I told myself that I would not play house with men, and would set this standard for my daughters. God is not through working on me."

"Life is a journey, and every day is an opportunity to overcome and better yourself."

Kanishia Wallace:

"Think like a Winner, Mind your mindset."

"God is often blamed for the negative things that happen to us and is usually given less praise for the good things in our lives. Fortunately, God is the beginner and the finisher. In every situation, good or bad, there is a message to be learned. Technically, everything that happens to us is a direct reflection on how we interpret things. If we believe everything in life is against us usually that's what we manifest into existence. We have no control over certain things in life, but we do have the ability to choose how we deal with every situation."

"There is something about enduring pain and going through changes in life that can bring a sense of victory and strength. It is important to understand, that no one is exempt from misfortunes. We all fall victim from time to time when situations present themselves and in order to regain control we have to decide to change our negative attitude immediately."

Sharice Porter:

"I was able to hear from GOD. I realized that through everything HE was right there. HE carried me when I fell. HE continued to build my strength back up. Without HIM I would not be here. There were times I wanted to throw in the towel. HE has given me the strength to endure. Although I have been through a lot, I continue to be patient and stand because I know that GOD isn't finished with me yet!"

Keilah Johnson:

"I never thought I would come out of my shell and talk about any of the things I have gone through or experienced. It took a lot for me to have the guts to share any of this. But one day I asked myself what benefit is it to stay in the dark? And what would I tell my younger self that would help her to become a better me? Had I known then what I know now, I probably could have avoided some major head on collisions in life."

Sharnice Evans:

"I have not allowed my emotions to dictate my actions. I have approached every conflict in a Godly manner. I am allowing God to work some things out in me during this very painful time in my life."

"You need to be encouraged in knowing that what has come to break you will only succeed in making you."

Denese Dilihant:

"I didn't have to compromise anything to be with him, he made me better in every area of my life. That's how I knew he was the one. He moved me and my son into his home, gave me his car and loved me like no one had ever loved me before. We prayed together, read scripture together, and our lives became nothing but love and ministry."

"He snatched me out of the darkness and literally made me to be a light to this dark world. It was during this time that I realized I could not take my sobriety for granted, even with all that I was now doing and how far I had come. I realized I had to wake up every morning and choose sobriety, choose life, and choose freedom."

"Rachel Edwards:

"Witnessing this great transition in this young women's life allowed me to see just why God allowed me to go through what I went through. If I had not gone through it I wouldn't be able to relate to what women in these circumstances go through and I would probably not have the drive and passion to help them. How could I be mad at God for giving me this opportunity to feel these women's pain and suffering up close and personal while assisting them, possibly saving their life?"

"I'm here to let my sisters know that nobody can validate them. In fact, you were beautifully and wonderfully made in God's image. There's nobody else like you in this world, so you see, there's no need for validation. One of the ladies in my writing group said "Pain is inevitable but suffering is optional.""

Mindset
Rehab
With Shamay Speaks

Download Shamay's
FREE
"Mindset Rehab" Audio & Workbook Today:
Visit :
https://payhip.com/b/SEXO
Or
www.ShamaySpeaks.com

BE ENCOURAGED AND TAKE CHARGE OF YOUR LIFE
FOR 2016.

Tell a friend! I hope this is the first step in changing your life
for the better. God Bless you on your journey!

Check out videos and more from Shamay:
www.Shamayspeaks.com
www.facebook.com/ShamaySpeaks
www.Youtube.com/ShamaySpeaks

144

Branches of Community Services
Tanicia Currie - CEO

communitybranches925@gmail.com

www.branchesofcommunityservices.org

(925) 709-4406 - Business Line

Tax ID #- Available upon request

Our Mission:

Our mission is to support the community by providing branches of educational support, resources, and opportunities for personal development. In fulfilling our mission, we hope to encourage the community to create a cycle of giving back to spread a message of universal community empowerment.

Speaker~ Author~Editor~Coach

"Serving steaming cups of inspiration for your soul + success"

Contact CoCo today!

www.CoCoSpeaks.net

E-mail: coco@cocospeaks.net

A Little About Coco:

About 10 years ago, I was the reluctant participant at one of my husband's music ministry youth outreach events. At the time of booking, the event planner asked my husband to share a brief story and to encourage the youth in attendance. My darling husband, happily and quickly suggested me for the task instead. His reasoning was that his gifting was music and I was a teacher with a lot of experience with youth so I was "well-equipped for the assignment." I guess he saw something in me that I didn't yet see in myself – a gift for public speaking.

Since that heart-racing, knee-knocking day, I have spoken at over 100 education workshops, women's conferences, youth and community outreaches, professional trainings, business seminars and faith-based conferences and retreats.

On a personal note, I have been happily married to my husband, Fil, for 15 years. He is my armor bearer, my best friend, my calm in the storm, and my biggest supporter (& public speaking launcher!). I have been blessed with two daughters. They are the wind beneath my wings. The three of them are my greatest joy. We live outside of Sacramento, California. In my free time, I enjoy reading, weight training, and road trips.

40004289R00095

Made in the USA
San Bernardino, CA
23 June 2019